Mr Stott's Diary - Halifa

Mr Stott's Diary

The Story of Life on the Home Front in Yorkshire during the Great War

Edited by Robert Hamilton

ISBN No 9781080736287

HALIFAX
GREAT WAR
1914
HERITAGE SOCIETY

Introduction

When members of the Halifax Great War Heritage Society first came across the diaries of William Henry Stott at an auction in 2013 little did they know the wealth of knowledge that they contained. Although we were unable to purchase them, we were fortunate that our member, Alan Rhodes, was able to ascertain they went to local historian, Stephen Gee, who very generously copied the years covering the Great War and gave them to us.

William was the owner of a small textile business and not a soldier or politician. He was writing his diaries for his own amusement and not for posterity and in them we found the views of the ordinary middle class man in the street. In this respect they are unique as he told us what he thought at the time without regard to the views of anybody else and without his thoughts being influenced by what people said later on. Consequently you get the true voice of what a man of his class and position in society really thought about events. He was also a talented artist and illustrated the diaries with cartoons and caricatures which greatly add to the richness of the content. As a man of his times his views and the terms he used reflect this, particularly with regard to race and gender, but in order to retain historical accuracy we took the decision not to censor them, even though some of his language and opinions would be considered offensive in this day and age. There has, however, been some editing to make the diaries more readable as William's use of grammar and punctuation could be quite eccentric at times.

William was born in Soyland, Yorkshire, in 1852. His mother died when he was aged only three which prompted his father, Henry, to move the family to West Vale, Yorkshire, where he set up a cotton twining and doubling business. Henry re-married in 1856 to Hannah Berry and three half siblings followed, Ernest 1862, Mary Hannah 1865 and Joe 1873.

By the time of the outbreak of the war, William had inherited the business, which was now located in Elland, Yorkshire, after the

death of his father in 1896. In 1888 he had married Martha Jane Ashworth (who he refers to as M J in the diaries) and they had two sons, Arnold born in 1890 and who unfortunately died aged 15, and William Ashworth born in 1894 who died in 1929 aged 35.
In 1924 the family sold up and moved to Carlton near Blackpool. William outlived both his sons passing away in 1935. He had diligently kept his diaries from 1872 until shortly before his death.

I would like to thank Elaine Beach, Graham Bradshaw, Patricia Morley, David Millichope, Alan Rhodes, Richard and Carla Spendlove, John Sunderland and Ann Wilkinson who gave so generously of their time to assist in the production of the diaries and their transcription from William's sometimes illegible handwriting, and all those who contributed in any way. In particular, thanks must go to Stephen Gee who so kindly gave us access to the diaries and, of course, to my wife Linda who tolerated my disappearance from family life for long periods while I was preparing the diaries for publication.

Robert Hamilton
Halifax Great War Heritage Society

1914

These days the Edwardian years are viewed as a golden era when Great Britain's empire was at its height and the country was enjoying an unparalleled period of stability and prosperity. In reality nothing could be further from the truth. Three great problems were afflicting the country and were threatening to tear the very fabric of society apart.

The first was the Irish problem. Perhaps to the surprise of some people who remember the troubles in Northern Ireland during the 1970s, 80s and 90s the issue has a much longer history. In 1914 the whole of Ireland was part of the United Kingdom. The predominantly Catholic south of the country wished to become independent and the Irish Parliamentary Party campaigned from 1870 for Home Rule. Home Rule Bills had been introduced by the Liberal Party in 1886 and 1893 but had been defeated in Parliament.

In 1911 a third attempt was successful but was vociferously opposed by the Ulster Unionists who wished to remain part of the United Kingdom. With the act due to become law in 1914 the Ulster Volunteers were formed and they began training and arming themselves in preparation to fight to retain their links with the mainland. To counter this the Irish Volunteers were formed in the South and it became increasingly likely that civil war would break out in the province. Even the British army, which traditionally did not get involved in political matters, became entangled in the issue with the so called 'Curragh Mutiny' when a number of officers declared that they would not fight against the Ulster Unionists in the event of hostilities between the two sides. The outbreak of World War 1 defused the tension with both sides putting their differences aside, temporarily at least, and the Bill being deferred for the duration of the war.

The second issue was the rise of the labour movement. In the early 20th century the United Kingdom was one of the richest countries in the world, but there was an enormous gap in wealth between the rich and the poor. Low wages, poor working conditions, long hours and an almost complete lack of employee rights had led to the formation of trade unions which were becoming more militant in their demands and were quite prepared to back them up with industrial action. The Independent Labour Party had been formed in 1893 followed by the Labour Representation Committee in 1900 which was renamed the Labour Party in 1906. The period between 1911-1914 has been dubbed by some as the 'Great Unrest' when millions of working days were lost to strike action across a whole range of industries. The situation became so tense in some areas, such as the South Wales coalfields and Liverpool, that troops were sent in and clashes occurred with the strikers resulting in a number of fatalities and a battleship appeared on the River Mersey. There was a genuine fear that revolution was in the air and the authorities appeared powerless to defuse the situation. It was only the start of the war which brought an end to the militancy when the unions agreed to call an end to the strikes in the spirit of national solidarity.

Last, but by no means least, there was the issue of women's suffrage. The campaign to gain women the vote had begun in the 19th century and in 1897 the various women's suffrage societies merged to form the National Union of Women's Suffrage Societies. They became known as the 'Suffragists' and, under the leadership of Millicent Fawcett, campaigned by peaceful and legal means to achieve women's suffrage. The pace of change however was slow, too slow for some members, and Emmeline Pankhurst and two of her daughters formed the Women's Social and Political Union who were to become better known as the 'Suffragettes'. Their motto was 'Deeds Not Words' and they lived up to it with a campaign of civil disobedience and direct action which included vandalism, arson, letter bombs and assault. The authorities retaliated by imprisoning their members and force-feeding them when they went on hunger strike. In August 1914 the Suffragettes, along with the other organisations mentioned above, suspended their activities for the duration of the war.

As for the war, there was not the jubilation on its outbreak as is popularly believed, but there was a determination to see it through and put the Germans in their place. The British sent their small army to France and it advanced into Belgium to meet the Germans at the town of Mons. Although they held off vastly superior numbers they were forced to retreat to avoid encirclement and it was only when they and their French allies were just north of Paris that they counter attacked at the Battle of the Marne and stopped the German advance in its tracks. After this each side moved northwards and tried to outflank the other. This so called 'Race to the Sea' culminated in the 1st Battle of Ypres between October and November when the Allies managed to beat off successive German attacks but only by a whisker and at a heavy price in the lives of their men. After this the trench lines, which were to become synonymous with this war, were formed between the Channel and the Swiss frontier and both sides were left to lick their wounds and ponder their moves for the next year.

Happy New Year

Let us keep our faces always towards the sunshine and the shadows will fall behind us (Whitman)

1 January

Cold day. Workpeople wanted to have holiday but persuaded them to keep on, while we have work in, we might have playing enough if trade does not alter.

2 January

Walked on to West Vale with Gilbert, called at J Nobles.

3 January

Hard day at mill, twiner off, this is the result of the Insurance Act, this man is in 2 clubs so he is as well off sick as at work, this the beneficial working of the biggest fraud that was ever palmed off on the public, they take a long time to effect a cure when they are in 2 clubs.

William is referring to the National Insurance Act 1911, introduced by the Liberal Government which ensured employees received sick pay and unemployment benefit.

4 January

Home all day

5 January

Trade very depressed all over the country, cotton just now is very bad indeed. I have my warehouse full, nobody wants anything.

6 January

The late Harry Beaumont left £19,158.

Female emigrants going out to Australia just now in great numbers.

7 January

Took Gilbert to Halifax tonight to look at the shops etc. We went to the pictures after "50 years of Queen Victoria"

Bills Bills Bills, still they come for the new machinery

etc etc, and with the slump in trade it's enough to drive one mad but it has to be fought.

8 & 9 January

Today paper announces the retirement of the Right Honourable Joseph Chamberlain one of the greatest politicians of our times. Gilbert isn't home this morning, it has been unfortunate that we should have had workpeople off and have had to leave him at home but he was no trouble and made the best of it, but I think he has enjoyed himself, we were pleased for him to come.

10 January

M J (William's wife Martha Jane) *went to see Mrs Rothwell. I stayed at home, roughed out postcard sketch, worked late at it.*

11 January

Cold day. Will went to Hx to meet Geoffrey Mellor who is touring with the Walty Dream Co and brought him to dinner and tea. I enjoyed his theatrical experiences. Mrs Rothwell and Mrs Mellor came to tea so we had a happy time

Strike in South Africa settled General Botha proclaimed Martial Law and squashed it in the bud, that's the proper way to settle strikes.

13 January

Board of Trade official opening the trams today, they start running regular tomorrow. Will went to Manchester for the first time on business. I cannot express what pleasure it gives us. I was held back by my Father, but I am not going to do so with my son, it's my duty to encourage him to the utmost and he starts with my wish for his success.

15 January

Opening day for the Huddersfield tram service, Coun Lumb drove the official car into Elland to the delight of thousands of spectators, this will be a boon to us it will open a new district to us although we are only 3 miles away, but the walk up Ainley has been a terrible drawback, of course this will be Halifax loss.

These were the first trams to run to Elland, Halifax Tramways having declined to extend their service. Trams ran every 15 minutes and tickets to Huddersfield cost 3d.

16 January

Will been to Manchester every day this week seeking business but nothing doing, things are wretched, you cannot give yarn, it made him downhearted poor lad, but better luck.

17 January

Very cold day. Halifax afternoon to matinee "Walty Dream" very good, Geoffrey Mellor is one of the Co. Met M J, Flora and Bertha after, had tea at Marsh's.

18 January

Wills 20th birthday, he took his mother to Oldham after dinner in the car.

19 January

Will went to Manchester again today with no better results, trade dreadfully bad, short time common in many parts, I felt sorry he was downhearted somewhat but he will try again.

20 January

Cold clammy day.

21 January

Will turned out again today and glad to say his efforts were successful for 20 Straps this will keep beans in the sack. I am delighted with his pluck and energy.

The usual strikes Blackburn, Burnley Corporation men but I think after the dousing they got at Leeds they will jack there.

22 January

Trade no better, hunted high & low but nothing wanted, all trades are feeling the depression.

23 January

Another airman killed, these fatal accidents keep happening although they can fly upside down the risk is still the same.

24 January

Wild wet night, Will went to Lindley. Stayed at home as usual, miserable.

25 January

Wild wet night, called to see J B Sutcliffe then went to Halifax to hear Will Owen lecture, he is a very popular black and white artist, he was very interesting.

26 January

Bitter, clammy, cold day.

27 January

All working today like niggers, my cold developed towards night and I went straight to bed, I was shivering.

28 January

Forced to stay in bed this morning, I was dead beat. I felt I could rest a month my bones ached that bad.

Trevelyan here tonight talking on the only topic he can talk about, Democracy. Of course he gets £1,600 per year to be able to talk this twaddle.

Charles Trevelyan was the Liberal MP for Elland and a champion of the working man. In 1914 no women and only approximately 2/3 of men had the vote. The Liberals had introduced radical legislation restricting the power of the House of Lords and guaranteeing sick pay and unemployment benefit.

29 January

Colne Valley Harriers today, they had capital sport, killed 2 and lost one, sorry I could not be with them, nothing does a fellow more good than a cross country.

30 January

Mr and Mrs Herbert Broadbent, our next door neighbours, were presented with a little daughter tonight, and all well.

31 January

M J went to Coley to Miss Greenwood, got simply soaked coming home. I went on town had difficulty, it was a perfect deluge with strong wind. I was glad to be at home.

1 February

The usual unpleasant weekend. I went to Birchencliffe Church to evening service, very reverent service, and I felt very happy and I shall go again.

2 February

No better trade.

3 & 4 February

Lord Derby offered his Bootle Estate for 1½ millions to Baron de Forest, of course it will result in nothing, he put on I see certain restrictions which any fool can see, which will nullify the bargain, it's simply a political vote catching job, it's like the above sketch of a well known advertisement, it's all cod.

Beautiful day very spring like.

5 February

Will distracted with tic, could not go to bed. I know what it is it's the D......

6 February

New twiner came today from Brighouse. I think he will be a good man, we want a more reliable man.

7 February

Huddersfield this evening with M J for the first time in the car, this will be very useful, but I think shopping is dearer but they have good choice, what a trade is done now in flowers, pink carnations, lovely hyacinths, really lovely but expensive.

8 February

In the afternoon Will took his mother to Todmorden in the sidecar. I stayed at home.

9 February

A day of anxiety at the mill, things persist in going wrong. We are still particularly waiting for business but nothing comes, we are getting very anxious.

10 February

Opening of Parliament today what the end of it will be goodness only knows, why not close it, we are now paying members £400 a year to keep the country in a turmoil.

11 February

We are all there thrashing through very stormy weather and all hands to the wheel.

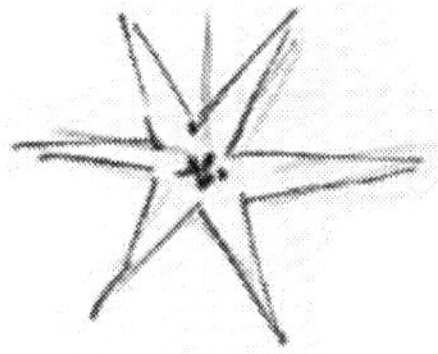

Time, Faith and Energy – the three friends God has given to the poor.

"Night and Morning"

Bulwer Lytton

12 February

Our unlucky star must be in the ascendency just now. All our work faulty and claims coming back every day, one of the effects of bad trade.

13 February

Dismissed twiner today, deliberately doing bad work, operators will not do their work right even if well paid, we are getting worse year by year.

14 February

Mr and Mrs Owen Street and Mr and Mrs Witham motored over from Oldham stayed tea, we were delighted for their short stay, because the road is very dangerous in the dark. Owen looking much better. Turned out a fearful wild night.

15 February

Blowing a gale all day

16 February

Mr Rothwell called this evening, came to see heard we were not too well, we were pleased to see him, he gave us great consolation on trade matters his sterling friendship we shall never forget

17 February

Cold raw day, night turned out a regular soaker. Heavy gales on the West Coast Morecambe suffered badly.

18 February

Marconi muddle on again, Lord Murray apologises but it is not yet finished.

The 1912 Marconi scandal involved claims that Liberal politicians profited from sales in Marconi shares as a result of inside information that the government was about to award a contract to the company.

19 February

Shopkeepers here say the trams from Huddersfield have improved their receipts, glad to hear it, well we found things much dearer at Huddersfield the other Saturday than they are at Elland.

20 February

Will went to Dempsters Dance. By all accounts it was a nice affair.

21 February

Will took his mother to Oldham in the afternoon. I took some flowers up to Greetland Church.

22 February

Restful day and God knows I require one. Joss came down afternoon too. M J to meet Will coming from Oldham, met him at Delph.

24 February

Raw day. We had the usual pancakes which were excellent. Shuttle Cock still begins at Shrove Tide.

25 February

The deported strikers from South Africa arrived today. Parliament in a fix on the Home Rule question.

The strikers rather dramatically depicted were the labour leaders who were forcibly deported from South Africa following a railway strike in January. They were welcomed by labour leaders in Britain and later allowed back to South Africa.

26 February

Sir John Tenniel, Punch's famous cartoonist died today, he had pictured History Weekly for 50 years. I simply worship his wonderful drawings and am familiar with all his well known ones. I had hundreds, the finest cartoonist the world has ever known.

27 February

Every day now shows the Insurance Act insolvent, all the Friendly Societies are on the verge of ruin. Lloyd George will now shift this loss on to the nation if the British are foolish enough to do it.

28 February

Bright day but cold. Harvey came about 3:30 alone, his friend could not come, after tea Will took him to Halifax they are great pals.

1 March

Will took Harvey for a run in the morning on the moors. Will and Frank went to Huddersfield in the evening to see him off.

2 March

Cold bleak day. Complaints every day, cannot do right.

3 & 4 March

Cold raw wind all day. G W Nicholson the well known Yorkshire humorist died today, he was very popular 20 years ago and sang at our concerts at West Vale. He once came to our house, I liked his style very much, he was clean in all his work, you cannot say that with many comic vocalists. He was better than many high salaried stars of the present day.

Punch Advice

Keep sober, single and a balance at your blankets

5 March

Poor Will, I feel sorry for him, he has worked like a nigger for months at those twiners in the new room, he has practically fixed them himself. The person we bought them from cannot do much at them and the brunt of the work has fallen on Will. He looks fagged with the worry and care.

6 March

Started one twiner in the new room today but made little progress but we were satisfied. I hope they will be beneficial to us.

7 March

We went to Coley afternoon to see Dr Jowett, found him very well indeed, but as usual full of work, he read to us the preface of a book on immortality which he will shortly publish, a very scholarly work.

8 March

Beautiful day and God knows we need it, we have passed through a troublesome week.

9 March

Home Rule Bill again before the House, they seem about full with it.

The Government were trying to introduce Home Rule for Ireland but it was such a controversial and divisive issue that there was a threat of civil war.

10 March

Sorry time in this evening's newspaper. The sudden death of Harry Fox only son of J Wm Fox late of West Vale who died out in China, he was about the same age as Arnold. We sympathise with them deeply in their hour of bitter sorrow.

11 March

Another complaint about work today, JWR. Our cup is almost full.

Military Station Bills O' Jacks situated above Saddleworth purchased by the Government, Wireless Telegraphy, 1600 ft high it has a western slope next to the mountains.

12 March

Got the last twiner running today. Will has done everything almost in the fixing up of them with the exception of levelling spindles etc. It is marvellous for a lad who 5 years ago a twiner was a stranger to him, his pride kept him up to the finish but he was completely done up, another week would have finished him, his pluck and determination should be rewarded. I feel proud to have such a boy.

14 March

Finished a most strenuous week, started cheese winding and we were behind time and we have all three worked hard and late to get up with the work. Will went to see Fred Terrys Co in the "Scarlet Pimpernel" at the (entry not finished)

15 March

M J went to Todmorden. I walked up to Greetland Church in the afternoon with flowers for Arnold.

Arnold was William and Martha's eldest son who had died at the age of 15 in 1906 and is buried in the family grave at St Thomas Church, Greetland, nr Halifax.

16 March

Cold day. Fearful gales on the coast and heavy floods in different parts. Will suffered torture all day and night with toothache or neuralgia.

17 March

R & J Holroyds mill on fire today, overheating of a shaft, they have sprinklers and well equipped with their own fire engine and they soon got it out but at one time it looked desperate

18 March

Trade still unsatisfactory although we are working all three for all we are worth, starting new business (cheesing) and behind time, they want it so fast.

Heated debate in the House on Home Rule, it looks like Civil War in Ulster.

19 March

Work difficult to please, we have had a bitter struggle to keep pace with complaints but we must say with a well known writer, J L ALLEN. Real struggle is itself real living and no ennobling thing on this earth is ever to be had on any other terms.

20 March

Will went to Manchester today to see Halliwell & Dearnley & Co about their account. They avoided seeing him, I am very dubious about them.

21 March

Spring came in today. Well we have not had a bad winter but we hail Spring. M J went to Miss Greenwoods.

22 March

Dull day. M J and Will went to Todmorden late afternoon, coming home they had puncture etc, I had quite a scare, did not come home until about 12 o'clock.

23 - 25 March

Sorry to see in tonight's paper the death of a very old friend of mine, William Rhodes of West Vale, in my salad days he was a boon companion. "Will" and I were good pals, he was a most generous, no vice, he was in much better circumstances than I was and gave me a lot of pleasure. I look back with no regrets through our long term of friendship, we had some happy times which are now faded memories. He never followed any business, his father left him well provided for. He leaves a widow and three children.

Grave crisis in Parliament on the Home Rule Bill. Troops drafted out to Ulster, resignations of officers in the army, expected dissolution over this infernal muddle.

26 March

Joe Noble came in this evening, told us about his visit to London.

27 March

Sharp, cold day. Very much upset over Halliwell & Dearnley not paying their account. J Crossley going to try to get it if possible

28 March

White frost this morning. Complaints again this morning.

29 March

Restful day

31 March

Paid £5 9s 10d Life Assurance.

1 April

M J and myself went to spend the morning with Mr and Mrs A W Law, Salterville, Halifax. This was the first time I had been to their new house, a splendid house, there were other friends there, after supper Mrs Walmsley sang and Mrs Law accompanied her and she also played some lovely pieces for us to our delight. Arthur was looking well and we had a good long chat, he is a capital host, he sent us back in a taxi. Mr and Mrs Witham there and also Mr George Normanton, had a jolly time.

2 April

Mr George Normanton sent a beautiful piece of cloth as a gift, it will make me an overcoat and M J one as well, it is very kind of him and we appreciate the gift very much

3 April

Dreadful cold in my head. 170,000 miners out in Yorkshire today, so we are face to face with serious loss to the community.

4 April

Went with Will in the sidecar to Grange Moor steeplechases, sort of pit mans Derby, the usual bookies were there and did good business. The racing was very tame what we saw.

5 April

Dreadful cold in my head stayed in bed till noon. Turned out a miserable wet afternoon. Ted came to tea.

6 & 7 April

James Mitchell better known in West Vale as "Little Jimmy" one of the best known characters in the village, a most ardent Radical and at the Shears it was well known the slightest slur at either Bright or Gladstone would bring Jimmy to his feet in a moment, we were good friends and I shall miss his familiar figure.

9 April

No settlement yet Yorkshire Miners who are out on strike. This is causing heavy loss to users of coal, some mills threaten to shut down.

10 April (Good Friday)

Few of the mills starting today, not from a religious point of view but in face of the coal strike.

11 April

Closed down today for the Holidays, it is very cold indeed and showery, poor look out.

12 April

Will took his mother to Blackpool in the sidecar, started at 6 o'clock fine but rather cold. I went to Todmorden by the 10 o'clock train. Will and M J got to Todmorden about 5:30. I came home with Will.

13 April

Todmorden today with Will. Mrs Eastwood came up in the afternoon and spent the evening with us and left at 8:45. We all stayed, very cold day.

14 April

Cold chilly wind. I went with J W to Townley Hall to look at the pictures, they were a very poor show. A capital exhibition of engravings by Sir Edward Landseer. I was disappointed but to visit this historical home to me is always a treat, having read the traditions of the House of Townley for here dwelt mighty hunters, brave knights, martyred priests, exiled reformers, sedate scholars and ladies fair. We all come home tonight after a pleasant weekend. Coldest Easter for a long time.

15 April

Started work again today. We all felt the effect of the holidays.

16 April

Sorry to see the death announced in today's paper of Mr Hubert Bland the well known journalist who for a long time wrote for the Sunday Chronicle under the name of Hubert. He was one of the original members of the Fabian Society, advanced Socialist,

Imperialist in the full sense of the word a devoted Roman Catholic, he was a charming personality. I was always fond of reading after him. In my opinion a cultivated man of the world, rich in the knowledge which comes of wide and various reading.

Hubert Bland was a contradictory character, a socialist who opposed women's rights and supported imperialism. He also fathered six children to three different women including his wife who was the author E E Nesbitt of "Railway Children" fame. It is surprising that William admired a man of such dubious morals.

18 April

Will took his mother for a ride and met Mr and Mrs Beattie on their machine, so they ran over Blackstone Edge and down the valley and back. They all enjoyed the run.

19 April

In the afternoon we had a run over to the Isle of Skye, highest public house in the country 1477 ft then to Bills O Jacks, Greenfield and then over to Stanedge.

20 April

Beautiful summers day, bright sun and very warm. Rode down to Mirfield with Will to see Mr Lister, saw a most beautiful sight, a fruit tree in full blossom. It looked as if it was covered in snow, it was most lovely.

21 April

United States at war with Mexico and about time, they have snubbed England and insulted the United States so they are getting their own back.

After an incident when nine American sailors were arrested the American navy occupied the port of Veracruz. The occupation ended six months later with the Niagara Falls peace conference.

22 April

Lovely day again. M J went on to West Vale in the evening to enquire about Mrs Joe Noble, glad to say she is better. King and Queen visit to Paris, they are giving them a royal reception.

23 April

Change in the weather, much cooler. Trade still depressed. Denton, the seat of the felt hat trade is practically at a standstill, workpeople nothing to do, soft hats and caps are now commonly worn.

24 April

Will not too well, these hard times hit him hard and he takes it to heart very much. He is too young to work I am sorry to say like he has done for the last 4 or 5 months.

25 April

Halifax tonight with M J to see "David Garrick" and the "Sleigh Bells", had a most enjoyable evening. Fair Co.

27 April

Started on the West Vale tram section today, they intend to be running for Whitsuntide. If they do it will be a marvellous feat of engineering.

28 April

Grave crisis in Ireland. Saw the new moon tonight, let us hope it will change our luck, had a most harassing day.

29 April

Sir Charles Doughty MP died, the Unionists have lost a most trenchant

Speaker. He was a rousing orator and the best I ever heard with hecklers. He was quick witted and never failed to bring down his man. I have heard him twice, once at Halifax and once at Elland.

30 April

Cold, frosty morning with a NE wind. West Vale tonight to see how Mrs Noble was, glad to say rather better.

1 May

Chilly breeze. Home Rule Bill, looks like some settlement has been arranged. Gilbert Robinson sails for South Africa, good luck to him.

2 May

Bright all day but cold E wind. Will took his mother to Todmorden in the car. I went to Halifax to have my hair cut. M J, after she got back, went to see Mrs Law and stayed to supper. Dr Potts brought her home, such a gentleman but lost, we are all sorry for him.

3 May

J Walters birthday, 66 all came down by morning train, a regular family gathering. Some of them went to Almondbury by tram, they enjoyed the outing very much.

4 May

Duke of Argyle died on Saturday.

5 May

Heavy loss in the Selby district, potato crop blighted owing to the frost of last week. 15 deg, this is estimated at £100,000.

6 May

Budget day. An election dodge taxing the wealthy to pander for the working man's vote.

7 May

Cold showery day. Anxiously waiting for a settlement from Halliwell & Dearnley & Co. Over £30 still owing since November.

8 May

Cold weather.
Lunatic in an asylum
Is that clock there right?
Dr, after comparing with his watch, Yes!
Lunatic, then what's it doing here?

9 May

Will and myself worked very late today to get a straight edge and when finished I was done up. M J went to see Misses Greenwood. Inflammation started in my left eye, very painful.

10 May

Dull, cold Sunday. Intended going to York midday Sunday. My eye much better but still painful.

11 May

West Vale tonight to see J Noble, glad to see Mrs Noble better. Huddersfield Corporation are working most strenuously to get the trams ready for Whit Week, all the road up from West Vale to Elland day and night.

12 May

Changing twiner again today, shall we ever be straight again.

13 May

Jack Whiteley, our new twiner, left today without notice. Well he has saved me the trouble of stopping him, he was a shirker. Just got the pair of twiners in the new room making a decent cop, it's been a struggle. Will has fought it hard and has conquered. It's a credit to a lad of his age and experience.

14 May

Shorthanded today, cannot tell where to turn for workers. Mr Albert Eastwood died this week, he was a well known business man.

15 May

Will not so well. The weather has altered this last few days, we are having a little sun just for a change.

16 May

Will took his mother for a ride this afternoon to Bolton Woods, Colne, Nelson and home by Todmorden, called at our folks. I had a good half day sketching a postcard. I can do this better when I am quiet and alone and can concentrate my thoughts better.

17 May

Beautiful sunny day, too hot to get out, but the fact was we were all too tired to make the exertion.

18 May

Got over black Monday very fair. Got a piecer but he is an old man but we are glad of that. I put an advert in 3 days, not a single applicant. Will went to Sowerby Bridge to settle up with Dugdales, £13 loss.

19 May

Poor Will had a terrible struggle today with the twiner, he could not get it to run right. We are much troubled about same.

20 May

Motor races started yesterday in the Isle of Man. The course was 18 miles and the winner did it at the rate of 45 miles per hour on an AJS. Very hot day, walked over the tram route to West Vale tonight, they are working hard to get finished by Whitsuntide and they will succeed. A wonderful piece of workmanship.

21 May

Hot, oppressive day. Heard the Corncrake tonight, first time this year, close to our house.

22 May

Suffragettes made a scene and insulted the King tonight at a Command Performance for a theatrical charity in London. Why not put them in a lunatic asylum. I wonder if this is a lonely woman that poets and painters have sung to us about. Shakespeare's wise lines are appropriate.

Lillies that fester smell worse than weeds

23 May

Started to sketch postcard for new trams to West Vale, they are very trying to do, it taxes you very much to get the right ideas. Got 1000 printed.

24 May

Never went out. Worked hard on a postcard sketch. I was tired towards night.

25 May

David Dutton was interred today. I never heard until I saw it in the paper this evening, he was one of the best known men in Elland, in business he was a canal carrier. He had a number of boats, a man who had seen much.

26 May

White frost this morning, I was horrified at 6 o'clock to see the fields and roofs all white, this coming after the warm weather and rain on Sunday, it made the plant life jump. It will have done countless loss to all crops. Cheshire farmers have suffered fearful losses.

27 May

Derby Day won by Durbar II, owned by a Frenchman, started 20 to 1.

28 May

Home Rule Bill passed the 3 reading. So here ends the Union of Great Britain and Ireland. What will be the fate of Ulster, time alone will tell.

29 May

Official opening of trams to West Vale. Board of Trade, Col Druitt, Coun Hamer of the Greetland Council drove an illuminated car from the boundary to terminus. I had a postcard out for the occasion. Another terrible calamity, the "Empress of Ireland" from Quebec to Liverpool was run into and sunk in 10 minutes, over a 1000 lives missing, too painful to read.

After the success of opening the tramline from Huddersfield to Elland, Huddersfield Corporation extended it to West Vale.
The RMS *Empress of Ireland* sank in the St Lawrence river after colliding with a Norwegian collier.

1 June

I went to Manchester this morning. I had not been there to look round since I left school. I went there, then after that to Peel Park Art Gallery then Belle Vue. I had J Noble for a companion and we enjoyed the day.

2 June

Will took M J to Bill O Jacks round by Oldham etc. in the afternoon I went for a run to Cawthorne a pretty place close to Common Hall.

3 June

Started work again, all went well for a wonder. Reading Wild Wales by George Barrow, a delightful book.

4 June

Buckingham Palace today. Some mad Suffragettes made a disgraceful scene in the presence of the King and Queen. It's about time something was done, they had got to the far end.

5 June

Cold day. Postcards selling fairly well.

6 June

Cold weather, Will took his mother for a ride to Todmorden but nobody at home so turned back. We stayed at home in the evening.

7 June

Still very cold, I stayed at home reading, sketching etc.

8 June

Cold, dull day. Will had 3 teeth drawn today at Halifax.

9 & 10 June

Soaking cold wet day, more like November than June. Trade still very dull, not only Cotton but the worsted trade is very bad. Nothing seems good, the country is full of unrest and we are face to face with a bad winter. Received a postcard from J Noble, been to Buxton with the Greetland Council by motor car.

12 June

Warm day but rather cold at night.

13 June

Beautiful hot day, Will and M J set off about 2:30 for Blackpool. I went to Halifax and just looked round then back home, bought a duplicate sketch block, I think it will be useful.

14 June

Beautiful bright sunny morning. Walked up to Greetland Church with flowers for Arnold and stayed for the service. Brought back happy memories. Will and his mother left Blackpool about 11:30, came onto Preston then Southport. Called to see Maud, stayed an hour then left for home. Landed about 7:30.

15 June

Beautiful day but very hot.

16 June

Cooler today somewhat but still hot in the mill.

17 June

Trade no better, everybody crying out. I am afraid we are in for a long spell.

18 June

J Noble had an accident in getting off a tram, slipped on the pavement and wrenched an ankle. All to oblige a lady.

19 June

West Vale tonight.

20 June

Over the hills to Junction then down Booth Dean to Ripponden. I had my first drive on the "Rex", I did fairly well. Bert Law came in his car for Will to stay with him for the weekend.

21 June

Thunder storm today, very heavy deluge. Will brought Bert Law visiting, they had been motoring in the hills.

22 June

Very heavy day.

23 June

Much cooler today. M J went to Todmorden yesterday and found them all very well. J W sent me a book, Tales for the Marines – Blatchford.

24 June

"Oppen thee math an shut, thee can see what God will send thee, that what they are to feel what a beeter way is. Oppen thee can and shut thee math. You'll face much better" – Bob Dubbs

25 June

Trade all round very bad indeed, Cotton is not the only trade that is slack but all seem to be alike, worsted, woollen etc. Halifax in the morning to see Mr Shaw about some spindles.

26 June

Very bad day. Joe Noble glad to say hopping about

27 June

Very hot day. Bertha came down this afternoon. Will took her for a ride. After that I went round Junction with Will and Mr and Mrs Rothwell. I had another go at driving.

28 June

Beautiful day. Will took Bertha to Oldham but they were away from home, they came back over Stanedge.

29 June

Very hot again today, had a most heavy day. It is reported that Vickers Co have acquired the controlling influence in the Low Moor Iron Works who for a century have been noted for their fine quality of iron.

1 July

Fearful thunder storm this afternoon, came very dark, the lightning was very vivid and a regular deluge. Many places were flooded, Bradford district suffered very badly, £100,000 is estimated. Messrs Edmund Sykes cleared out today from Owlet Hall Mills, they have gone to Krumlin Mill, Scammonden. I wish them success. Heatons have behaved so I hear.

2 & 3 July

Most oppressive day, we are all done up. Will sorry to say much run down, we are much concerned.
Death of Joseph Chamberlain from 1876 to 1914 was MP for Birmingham. His career in the realms of imperial politics was indeed a very dazzling one and one of the greatest men of his time. M J reading "Night and Morning" – B Lytton, likes it very well.

4 July

Went to Coley with M J to tea at the Vicarage, found Dr Jowett very well. After tea he took me to the church to see the new stained window recently put in by Mr Wilkinson, a very beautiful window, another will be put in next week.

5 July

Over Blackstone Edge to Todmorden with Will this afternoon, we sat down and admired this beautiful moorland to our hearts content.

7 July

Bright day and not too hot. Most anxious day, we are full up with stock, nothing wanted, cannot move in the place and what's more nothing for it, we cannot endure this strain much longer.

8 July

Received letter of congratulations from B & J Sutcliffe. Arthur Ackroyd, Travellers Rest died today suddenly. Poor Arthur, I am truly sorry, human nature can only stand a certain amount of strain.

9 July

Sent B Sutcliffe congratulations to the accompanying sketch.

10 July

Halifax in the morning to get my hair cut, came straight back. Motor cycle trials in this district today, they have found some of our hills too much for them.

11 July

Will off to Oldham for the weekend, gone solo.

12 July

Blackpool with M J for the day, Mr and Mrs Bert Robinson there. Turned out a wet afternoon, it was very busy. Left at 7:50 got back comfortable at 10:15.

13 July

Close oppressive day. Received postcard from Flora and Bertha, gone to Redcar for their holidays. Been to Staithes, Runswick etc. They like it very much, who would not in such a picturesque county like that.

14 July

Much troubled over Will, he found his hair falling off in patches. The doctor thinks it's weakness, gave him some medicine. We do hope he will soon be alright, there is no doubt he is very much run down.

15 July

Reading a capital novel by Miss Braddon, she has a style that rivets your attention and in these racking times diverts your attention and makes you live as if you were in another sphere of life for a time.

16 July

Warm weather. M J got a new bonnet

17 July

Dull showery day

18 July

Will ran over to Oldham to fetch Harvey this afternoon to spend the weekend. I went to West Vale and called to see J Sutcliffe, sorry to find Mr B not so well.

Very hot week

19 & 20 July

Sorry to record the death of our very old friend Mrs Shaw. She was on a visit to Manchester when she had a seizure and never recovered. For over 20 years she was a constant visitor, she came to help M J with her needlework. She formerly was a dressmaker and since we came to Elland where she lived she used to come to our house at all times just like coming home, she lived by herself and since her son died, poor woman, she never seemed to get over it. She was a staunch church woman and always stood by it. She was very kind to us, she at any time would come to help in any way. I used to like her to come, she could tell all the pedigrees of everybody in the village. Capital memory, nobody will miss her more than at our house. She was very fond of Will and he will miss her much.

21 July

Record day for heat.

22 July

M J attended the funeral of our old friend Mrs Shaw at Elland Cemetery, Mrs Eastwood and Hilda came.

23 July

Will consulted a hair specialist at Oldham on Monday, says he will put him right in a few weeks. His Majesty called a special meeting of the Premier and others to try to bring some common sense into the Home Rule question. To have to bring the King into this question is a disgrace to this Radical Government.

24 July

Change in the weather, rain fell and it turned bitter cold. Mr Ramsden, the Unionist candidate, addressed a meeting in the square along with other speakers, Mr Hamer made a capital speech.

25 July

Very cold boisterous day. Went to West Vale with M J, saw her uncle Tom.

26 July

Mrs Eastwood came to tea this afternoon, stayed until evening. M J and her had a long talk about our old friend Mrs Shaw.

27 July

Change in the weather, much cooler. Norwegian airman flew from Scotland to Norway, 325 miles. This is the longest over sea record yet.

28 July

Fall in cotton.

29 July

War declared between Servia and Austria, this might bring other powers into action and England might become involved but let us pray against this, we have enough on at present, Strikes, Unrest and

Ireland. Went on a ride with Will tonight around Krumlin Mill and the Brown Cow, it was very chilly.

The first mention of the crisis in Europe. As you can see William felt there were more pressing domestic issues to consider. This entry reflected feeling in the country at the time.

31 July & 1 August

Greatest excitement prevails. Russia orders general mobilisation and attacks Austria. Martial Law proclaimed in Germany. Money crisis, Bank Rate soars from 4% to 8%, Stock Exchange closed. Mr Asquith, in the House of Commons, said Europe govs all realise that there is no hope now to localise the war. Every nation is making strenuous efforts to be ready to throw herself into battle so we are face to face with a crisis unparalleled this century. Parliament voted £50,000,000 for war expenses.

2 August

Special editions were issued today. Germany crossed the frontier and occupied Luxembourg thus breaking the Treaty.

3 August

Government closed the banks for 3 days. Great scene in the House of Commons today, Sir Edward Grey gave a masterful speech and order given to mobilise the army today and the navy to clear for action and if war really starts we are in duty bound for our own shores to stand by France and protect her shores from this mad Emperor. For 20 years they have plotted to get nearer to us and this is a bold stroke of his but he will find out his foolish mistake.

5 August

11 o'clock last night war was declared against Germany, the greatest excitement prevails. Benzol last week was 1/2d per gallon this week they are wanting 3/- so cannot afford to run our motor sidecar at present owing to the War Authorities stopping sale of Benzol as they use it for explosives etc.

6 August

HMS Amphion ran onto a sunk mine and was blown up, this our first loss. The Belgians at Liege repulsed the Germans with a loss of 25,000, this is a wonderful stroke for the little Belgians.

HMS *Amphion* had pursued and sunk the German minelayer SS *Konigin Luise* on the 5 August and then later in the day sank after striking one of the mines she had laid. 150 of the crew and, ironically, 18 German survivors were killed. At Liege the Germans suffered the first delay to their plan to defeat France.

7 August

No particular news today, the papers are very reticent about giving news because it soon gets to the enemy. Our neighbours Mr and Mrs Jagger have 3 sons off to camp.

8 August

We closed today for a week maybe longer, some mills standing a fortnight. In fact trade is at a standstill. Expected Bertha but did not come.

9 August

Irving Holt and Walker, two of our Will's pals join the "Terriers", they called to say goodbye, we wish them luck.

10 August

I went with Will to Blackpool along with the brothers Graham, we had a bad run several punctures on the road which delayed us. At Preston we saw a large force of Terriers going on active service with all their horses, vans and ammunition vans etc. It was a very interesting sight, we stayed with Mrs Robinson – Blackpool fairly busy. Ma went to Todmorden.

11 August

Will and Joss went to Windermere. I came home with Charles in their car, we had a lovely run, stayed a time at Whalley, most interesting, then ran onto Mitton and looked through the ancient church, shown the Sherburne Monuments, the once Lords of

Stonyhurst but the line ran out, the heir died then the place was empty a long number of years, then the Jesuits took it and they have been in possession of it for 120 years. We then ran forward to the stately pile Stonyhurst College, one of the highest Catholic colleges in the country. It is an imposing building and situated in a lovely position. I have long wished to see Stonyhurst of which I have read so much but today I have had my wish gratified. Called at Todmorden and had tea, there I came on home with Charles.

12 August

Will and Joss got home from Windermere about 4:30, they had enjoyed the outing very much. They came home by Settle, Skipton etc. etc. in about 6 hours.

13 August

Will took his mother to Heptonstall and had tea there, then forward to Holme Chapel but had tyre trouble which delayed them.

14 August

Joss called, I went round the moors to Nont Sarahs, stopped on the moor, it was very enjoyable. No news of the war, troops are massing on each side and daily expect to hear of a dreadful battle. Trade at a standstill.

15 August

Everybody playing today. Great many mills standing next week, the outlook very black as all Europe now seems at arms. This will be the hardest struggle England has had, the Germans with their huge army will take some quelling and will entail thousands of lives and millions of money.

16 August

Afternoon we all went to Malham. I rode with Joss, Will took mother. It was a delightful day via Keighley and Skipton. After tea we walked up to Gordale Scar, a very grand site. Had a good run home but had a near shave with a motor car, got home at 6:45, all pleased with the outing.

17 August

Started work this morning but for how long cannot say.

18 August

We are the only cotton mill running this week in Elland but are only running up what stock we have in. No fresh news from the seat of war, great secrecy is excusable in this matter. Lord Kitchener put a stop to all war correspondents until the censor passes the word.

19 August

British troops, 150,000, have been landed we are told without a single casualty, our wishes and prayers go with them. Germans are massing their troops in a long line. Prince of Wales Fund, National Relief Fund amounted today to £1,375,000.

20 August

Belgians have gone to Antwerp, what this move is we cannot say. Pope of Rome died today, he will be known as the peasant pope, the horrors of this war seem to have hastened his end. His last words were the Almighty in his goodness wishes to spare me the horrors which Europe is undergoing.

21 August

Germans occupied Brussels, to avoid them shelling this historical place they retired to Antwerp. No special war news. Most mills cotton, worsted standing this week, most trying times. I am afraid we are going to have a bitter struggle for existence for a time.

22 August

Bertha came today and we had a beautiful run into Wharfedale. Bolton Woods and then to Burnsall, this I consider a lovely place, had tea there. I rode with Charles, Will took Bertha, left here 3 o'clock got home about 9. So ended a delightful day. Brussels occupied by the Germans.

23 August

Restful day. Will received a letter from his pal Frank Buckley, gone to join the colours.

24 August

Today reports British troops in action. Fall of Namur. Japanese bombard Tsing-Tao. The most stupendous struggle in history has commenced in Belgium but the Belgians have fought like heroes.

25 August

Lord Kitchener made a splendid speech in the House of Lords tonight, how well men had enrolled to the colours since he asked for more troops, he said we must have more still. Our colonies have offered both men and money, Germany has all her troops in the field, no reserve to fall back on, we must have a reserve to fill up the ranks, our Empire is at stake.

26 August

Report today, battle in Belgium, our troops are in the fighting line and we lost 2,000 but the enemy lost more than this. Russians in East Prussia and pushing forward and have gained a decisive victory. Heavy fighting in Belgium, the Germans are trying to break the combined armies by a huge blow so both sides suffered heavy losses.

27 August

Great progress is being made at the Barracks, a rush to join the colours. Victoria Hall used for sleeping etc. also other large schools etc. Cars all placarded, Join the Colours and Save the Empire etc. etc.

28 August

Dr Jowett came to tea, he was looking well and in good spirits. He is Lieutenant Chaplain to the reserves and might have to go to the front. Naval battle off Heligoland, sunk 5 German cruisers.

29 August

All cotton mills are practically stopped, best of them doing 3 days per week. Went to Greetland Church with flowers for Arnold, then to Halifax. Will went to York this afternoon with his Ma, they had a good run there but tyre troubles coming home, got home safely at 8:30.

30 August

At death grips in northern France, heavy losses.

31 August

Today's news comes, superb heroism of British troops, glorious stand in 4 days fighting, losses between 5,000 and 6,000. Brilliant work in the naval battle off Heligoland, 5 German ships sunk.

The talk of a four day stand was optimistic. A brief respite of one day had been gained at Le Cateau after which the retreat southwards continued. The naval battle of Heligoland was a minor skirmish which sank four German ships with no losses on the British side.

1 September

For 3 days the Germans have tried to break through Anglo French line but without success. Rapid recruiting going on all over the country at a rapid rate, a battalion at Liverpool was completed in half an hour.

2 September

Our losses to present are over 10,000, one of our Yorkshire Regiments have lost a large number of officers and men, they are in the thick of the fighting. Poor Belgium has suffered terribly, the barbaric Germans have burnt and murdered women and children, the passion of the civilised world is roused at this devilish work.

3 September

Allies falling back, the enemy are going forward to Paris but in this I hope they will be disappointed. Trade at a standstill we have only had a pair of twiners running this week, the pair in the garret and the odd twiner has stopped. Cannot get anything, we are all much depressed at this.

4 September

French Government move from Paris to Bordeaux for safety, we shall hear of something serious in a day or two. I think the Allies have something in store for them.

5 September

Will took his mother to Todmorden over Blackstone Edge but found no one at home so came back. Mr Street called this afternoon in our absence, we were sorry. Germans seem bent on getting through the line to Paris, I hope they will be frustrated. Hull Liner ran onto a mine and was lost also many trawlers. They must have laid hundreds.

6 September

Will ran over to Oldham to see Harvey, he was stranded coming back at Outlane, tyre burst. M J and myself went to service at West Vale. Mr Richardson preached a most excellent sermon on the war.

7 September

I had to go home this afternoon with lumbago. I could not do anything, quite helpless, went to bed. Germans falling back from Paris.

8 September

Only 1 pair of twiners running, we are all much depressed, no work offered at all, many of our friends in the same trade stopped altogether, Brighouse at a standstill. Halifax enrolling more men to the colours than they can accommodate, the same all over the country.

9 September

Indian troops will be landed now in a few days, 3 divisions, they are also sending money as well. Native Princes are coming to fight with their troops. Are we downhearted, I should think not.

"Make no mistake this is a fight to the finish if we go under now we go under forever" – Lord Rosebery.

10 September

Coley church tonight to hear the Bishop of Knaresborough preach the Harvest Festival, M J could not go with me. He spoke on the war. German troops falling back all along the line, our troops are doing gallant work.

The Allies had successfully counter attacked on 5 September on the Marne forcing the Germans to withdraw. This was a turning point of the war. The German plan to defeat France before turning on Russia had failed.

11 September

Premier's statement. 1,200,000 for the field exclusive of the overseas aid. 439,000 recruits in a month. Cotton trade still paralysed.

12 September

Allies still making progress. Will and Ted Buckley went to spend the weekend at Oldham.

13 September

Reading "For the Term of His Natural Life" by Marcus Clark, a book that 20 years ago thrilled one. I have never forgotten it, its description of convict life is horrible but true but it's well written. Dumas never wrote better.

14 September

My teeth this last four weeks have caused me much pain. I have had the most excellent set up to the present but it's getting fast to the gum period.

15 September

Encouraging news from the seat of the war, our troops are steadily driving the Germans back.

16 September

Warp Heads annual outing.

Sawley Abbey. The situation is lovely but the sketch here shown is about all that is left, there are traces of the walls close by.

17 September

Felt somewhat stiff today with our outing yesterday but buckled to with my work. What little we unfortunately had to do.

18 September

Woollen trade very brisk. Khaki orders are being done in the neighbourhood also army blankets are heavily booked for some time to come.

19 September

Standing today, Will and M J ran to Rochdale, Bacup and Todmorden, called at John Walters.

20 September

Cold day but fine

21 September

Severe fighting at Aisne but the Germans are giving way but losses on both sides are heavy. The cultured Germans shelled Rheims Cathedral with all its historical relics etc. and it is now in ruins, this must be revenged by all means.

22 September

Today brings bad news, 3 British cruisers torpedoed with heavy loss of lives off the Hook of Holland.

23 September

Got some 60 ft today from Holroyds, this will put us on another week or two. No better news in the cotton trade, still stagnated. Will received a letter today from Frank Buckley, he has joined the 2nd Battalion Royal Fusiliers and is training at Epsom, he seems to be having a rough time in camp.

24 September

Woollen trade and worsted trade are busy, some running overtime on Government work. M J, sorry to say, not so well.

25 September

Cotton still at a standstill. Manchester reports from bad to worse with no Liverpool market. All the mills are now anxiously waiting, nothing at all doing.

26 September

We worked today. Saw the Whistling Collier that used to come to West Vale 12 or 14 years ago, he only plays for certain customers in every village. I had a talk with him, he was going to Lindley, he said he had a few customers there. He always called at Heatons.

27 September

West Vale Church Harvest Festival. Dr Jowett preached in the afternoon. Mrs Law and Miss Law and Mrs Eastwood were there, they came on to our house for tea then we all went back to evening service. Mr Richardson preached, the decorations were very neat, a Union Jack was worked in flowers and hung against a pillar with all the names of the soldiers who have gone to the front, 42. The font was lovely, Miss M Law never did it better.

28 September

Geoffrey Mellor called today, he is playing this week in Huddersfield in "The Attack"

29 September

Mrs Law and Mildred took the beautiful cross from the font along with flowers and took them to Greetland Church and placed them on dear Arnold's grave on the anniversary of his death. She wrote us a letter telling us this, a most beautiful letter (Mrs L is a past master in writing), we are overwhelmed with gratitude at this kind remembrance, words fail me to say more.

30 September

First military funeral here today. Private Hardcastle died from wounds at Mons. Soldiers from the barracks, coffin on gun carriage and the band playing, it was most impressive.

1 October

West Vale tonight with M J. Patriotic Concert promoted by Miss D Waller and Miss Briggs. It was a capital concert in every respect. Mr Teal tenor, Mr Hodgson baritone and Mr Mallinson sketch. The proceeds amounted to £50 for the Belgian Refugees and Local War Fund, we thoroughly enjoyed it, saw lots of friends.

Almost immediately after war broke out, distress and comforts funds were started to support the troops and their dependants. This patriotic concert was just one of many that took place all over the district to raise money.

2 October

Lit up at the mill for the first time tonight, our landlord is running until 8 o'clock with khaki.

3 October

Will went to Huddersfield Theatre to see Geoffrey Mellor in "The Attack". He got behind to his dressing room, he took his part splendidly.

4 October

Fine day M J went to Mrs Rothwells. I walked up in the evening, they had two lady visitors from London but by their sparing dresses I don't see where ladies come in. It strikes me that we are getting back to the Garden of Eden before the fall (bah).

5 October

Russian great victory over the Germans in East Prussia. Desperate battle still raging with a far flung battle line but we are still plodding on I hope to victory.

6 October

Finish stretching the pair of twiners in the garret, they were never half set up in the beginning. When trade does revive I shall be ready, if ever it does. Lancashire spinners getting their back up at the Liverpool Cotton Brokers over closing the Cotton Market, they intend ignoring them and buying direct, why not, if any profit let those who work it have it, not them that gamble with it.

7 October

Got some 2/18 pin cops today from J W Rothwell also 3/14 from Holroyds. They are for tents for the government. It will be hard work but thankful for this.

8 October

Germans shelling Antwerp, this will cause consternation all over the world. No city contains such architectural beauties as does Antwerp. Man's inhumanity to man makes countless thousands mourn. Burns was wrong here he should have said Woman's.

9 October

Beautiful day. Nothing today much from the seat of war, only the ruthless burning of art work, their chief objects are churches and Antwerp contains some of the most beautiful churches in the world.

10 October

Miss Greenwood of Hipperholme came to tea this afternoon, Frank Booth and his friend from Oldham came for the weekend, our Bertha here as well, we had a jolly time.

11 October

Beautiful day, Harry Father turned up in the afternoon with Mr Winterbottom, motored over, our first experience of Mr W. capital singer he sang "Come into the Garden Maude" and others. They did not stay to tea they were anxious to get back before dark.

12 October

War news still depressing, Antwerp in the hands of the Germans and Ghent now threatened. It looks very black, aeroplanes are still flying over Paris and dropping bombs, one dropped on Notre Dame.

13 October

Hard day at mill, 1 twiner on 2/18s pin cops, doffing about 5 times a day. Belgium's refugees are being housed in many places around here.

14 October

Grave crisis in the cotton industry, Lancashire just now are in a bad way, some large mills stopped entirely, most only doing 3 days a week. A deadlock between Liverpool and New York seems inexcusable, there is a difference of 1½d per lb. Beautiful weather, the banks are financing the brokers to help them to tide over this trouble at the expense of those who have to work the staple article, this is morally wrong.

15 October

HMS Hawke was sunk today by a German submarine. Annie Briggs married, her husband is going on foreign service. Germans now occupy Belgium, Ostend is invaded, they are evidently pushing to the seaboard but for what idea no one seems to know.

16 October

Recruiting is the chief topic and I am pleased to see the country coming forward in such a noble manner, we shall need all we can get to tackle this German demon.

17 October

M J went to Miss Greenwoods for tea, I could not get away early enough. Tonight's news says we have sunk 4 German destroyers.

18 October

Beautiful day, more like June.

19 October

Better news today from the front, we are slowly driving the enemy back. The Russians now are getting to grips and have captured many prisoners and guns. General French's despatches are published today.

20 October

We are fagged today, these hard times we have to work shorthanded to make it pay at all and it's terribly hard changing counts every other day. Nothing straight forward and losing money at the same time but we are living and we must be thankful. We shall have our reward sometime.

21 October

St John's, West Vale "At Home". Mr and Mrs Geo Normanton host and hostess. M J and myself went on, we enjoyed the evening very much, old faces were glad to see us. Germans trying to get to the coast but the Allies keep pushing them back. They have got to Ostend but the English fleet have shelled them and they are falling back, the same from Antwerp so on the whole our position, as the authorities say, is satisfactory.

22 October

No time for sketches, work and reading, the war news takes all our attention

23 October

Kitcheners Army marched from Halifax to Elland headed by the band, they were recruits and are training. They looked a fine lot of young fellows. I felt like taking off my hat to them as they passed. I felt so proud that we still have the same old patriotic spirit left. Will very ill all day, we are very anxious.

24 October

Matinee - Royal Halifax, "Marriage Market", it was splendid. Good all round Co and some capital acting. Ted Buckley, our Wills companion, who was apprenticed to Messrs Dempsters is leaving to take a position as Under Foreman in the Gasworks at Farnham, we are all very sorry he is going away, they have been the best of pals and we all feel the break very much, especially Will, he was much distressed to lose his companionship and it was a great trouble to him. In fact there was no difference in their affection but all our best wishes go with him in his new

position and we wish him the best of health and good luck.

26 October

Many Belgian refugees are coming in the neighbourhood, many come to Halifax etc. People are giving up their houses for them, poor Belgium happy, prosperous now laid in ruins.

27 October

Germans trying to get to Calais but have been held back with terrible losses.

28 October

Better news today, the Allies are making good headway. Got a few straps 2/20 ww, this will take a week on 1 twiner so just now have all running. Another steamer sunk off the N of Ireland, ran into a mine, they must have laid thousands, what have we been doing to let them.

29 October

Dull day. M J went to Mrs Law to tea. Will went to fetch her back. German revolt in South Africa looking very serious, this is another Kaiser surprise but glad to see the S A Government are taking active steps.

30 October

Another surprise packet this morning, Turkey have been threatened by the Germans to blow up the palace by the 2 German warships that have run to Turkey for shelter and Turkey in a fit of madness promises to help them. If so this will wipe Turkey off the state of Europe.

31 October

Dull miserable day. Heavy fighting in Flanders the enemy is pressing for all it is worth to get to the coast but they get no nearer but the losses are heavy. Russians are now making themselves felt and have inflicted heavy losses on the Germans around Warsaw.

1 November

Reading Abbe Dimnet's "France Herself Again", shows how materialism and malhumanism have weakened France but he argues that this is past, they have seen their folly. They have been like many of our milk and water politicians who have squabbled for years on pettifogging Bills instead of looking to the nations welfare, patriotism means attention to the position of ones country.

2 November

Red Cross steamer wrecked off Whitby owing to all the lights on the E coast being put out.

3 November

Still desperate fighting, the enemy attempting to get to the coast of France but each time are repulsed with heavy losses.

4 November

Recruiting still going on, the Government have lowered the standard for height somewhat and this will bring in thousands more. Halifax 33 Regiment have raised their full number but it's been a very hard task. Papers are full of hints we are to have conscription, I hope not, we can get men if we pay them and surely England the mightiest nation of the world can do this. Naval battle off Chile, HMS Monmouth was sunk and crippled two others. Five German cruisers attacked them, we were outclassed with guns. John Shaw Gaunt a Manchester yarn agent for 50 years failing is £32,000.

5 November

Russian army coming west slowly but with reasonable effect, fighting around Cracow, they have simply mowed down their opponents. They will soon be at Vienna and Berlin then the climax will come, the Kaiser cannot cope with both ends, would to God it was now.

6 November

Woollen mills working overtime on Government work. Clothing, blankets etc. Doublers cotton are more or less at a standstill and will be bound to ruin many this long stoppage. Mr Hoyle of Brighouse who did a big business with Germans has lost a lot of money and called a private meeting.

7 November

M J and Will took flowers to Greetland this afternoon for Arnold. Walked up to Mr Rothwells evening, stayed for supper. A most trying week for work for all of us at the mill but thank God we have that.

8 November

Dull day. Will took his mother this afternoon to Oldham, got back just before dark, came by Ripponden.

9 November

Kitcheners words somewhat cheer us today. We can rely on our ultimate success. No time for sketching up log when I got home, I feel too tired to do it but we must stick until better times. We sometimes feel as if we would throw up the sponge.

10 November

Good news today, the "Emden" the German armoured cruiser which was in the Indian Ocean (and) has taken and sunk 20 vessels, estimated value £2,000,000, was captured and sunk by an Australian Cruiser.

11 November

Severe fighting still continues in Belgium, the Germans keep hurling huge armies to break through to the coast, but are repulsed at every trial at a cost of life which is dreadful to think of. We are fagged with work, all at home are trying our best to help in every way to lessen the cost of running at this critical time of little work at a little pay. We ought to be rewarded sometime, 6 to 8 for weeks has been our portion.

12 November

Sir Walter Gilby dead, began life with a penny in his pocket and rose to a huge business, S W Gilby Wine and Spirit Merchants, was a famous horse breeder too. A great friend of the late King Edward.

13 November

Total British Casualties 57,000

101 day of War

Russians making great progress in East Prussia, they say they will be in Berlin Xmas if not before.

14 November

Halifax this morning to the Arts Croft Annual Exhibition, not quite as large as usual but the quality of work very good. I was much impressed with the work, had a long chat with R E Nicholson an old artistic friend, he wanted me to be a member. Sorry I have not the time to devote to this object I dearly love.

15 November

Surprised this morning. Nature had attacked herself in her winter shroud but towards evening it began to thaw, home all day reading a delightful book by Halliwell Sutcliffe by Moor and Fell in West Yorkshire. The Bronte country has a large share, very well written and some very beautiful drawings of that district.

16 November

Lord Roberts died on Saturday, Commander in Chief, he had gone to France to inspect the Indian troops at the front, caught a chill and died. Had the nation taken notice of him years ago we should have been better prepared.

Field Marshall Lord Roberts (1832-1914) was one of the most successful British commanders of the 19th Century. He was one of only two non-royals to lie in state in the Palace of Westminster, the other being Winston Churchill.

17 November

Heavy fighting in Flanders but the enemy makes no progress the slaughter is terrible.

18 November

Russians slowly but surely coming west and are inflicting heavy losses on the enemy. Belgian refugees come to Elland. War loans issued £350,000,000. Khaki weavers in this district and working till 8 and 9 o'clock, cannot get it out fast enough.

19 November

Cotton Mills here are still very slack most of the doublers who were doing continental trade have had to pick up all kinds of work 18s 20 24 26s. Some have lost all their workpeople owing to the long stoppage.

20 November

Lord Roberts buried today at St Paul's. Passing of a great soldier with military honours. The King present, 8-10,000 present. Cold foggy day, taxes for the war, budget day. Tax on tea and our old favourite beer comes in for another tap, is patriotism peculiar to him, it looks like it.

21 November

Joffre, the French general has issued the following notice to his troops. No ladies admitted to the trenches whether on business or pleasure. The French have a funny way of expressing themselves. Went to Coley to tea to Dr Jowett, he had been to Buxton for a fortnight and was looking very well, had an interesting chat about the war, he was rather optimistic.

22 & 23 November

Cold dull day. Sorry to record of the death of Herbert Fox of West Vale who for 32 years was the organist at St John's. I was intimately acquainted with him most of the time. His father was the organist at Greetland for 32 years, he was a good musician and a good teacher. Arnold was under him a long time. He was musical conductor of all our concerts etc. and prominent in our minstrel troop. Poor Herbert how he will be missed.

24 November

Keen cold wind. Our brave fellows at the front are feeling the cold blast of winter, our hearts go out to them, fighting bravely for our prestige and crushing out this German military despotism. We shall do it but to what cost of money and lives, it is horrible to think of but I think it will bring peace for a very very long time when finished.

25 November

Attended the funeral of Mr Herbert Fox at Greetland church. Dr Jowett, Rev. Marshall and Rev. Richardson, all the vicars he had been under. The church was packed, the choir sang God is a Spirit. Dr Jowett came on to our house to spend the evening.

26 November

Dull wet day. Naval disaster off Sheerness, 800 lives lost, HMS Bulwark blows up.

27 November

Great Russian victory in East Prussia. M J went to Mrs Eastwood's she has been very badly we were sorry to hear. Harry Waller JP lost his trial in London with George Garside, I am glad.

28 November

One way to unsettle a question is to argue about it. No one would think there was a war going on at all, people do not seem to realise it yet, all places of amusement are in full swing and they don't seem to care. If they would only try to think of poor Belgium.

29 November

King George went to the seat of war today to Sir John French 170 years since a sovereign went to the front amongst his troops in time of war.

30 November

Heavy rain. Germans are still trying to break through the lines to get to Calais, they are said to have 120,000.

The 1st battle of Ypres had ended in stalemate. The trenches now stretched from the English Channel to the Swiss frontier. Activity continued with small local attacks.

1 December

Fearful gusts of driving rain at intervals all day. Cotton trade is said to be improving, some branches are very busy, heavy stuff for the government. Hebden Bridge ready-made clothiers cannot cope with orders and are badly off for workpeople.

2 December

Mr Ackroyd our neighbour, cotton spinner – sale of machinery today his lease is up at the mill and the bad trade and trouble with getting workpeople, he's pulling out. I wish I could, it gets worse every year, you cannot get people to work they want a loose job now. In Poland the Germans are said to be conducting a perilous retreat.

3 December

De Wet, the rebel, run to earth and captured.

4 December

New twiner today, well one we have had before, Thomas Midgley, we had too much to do ourselves and the other man we had was no organiser, which made it too difficult for Will, so we hope to do better work and more of it.

5 December

Had the most dreadful week for heavy rain and high winds, tonight it was very bad, heavy lightning. Reading, when time, "The Compact" by Rex Beach and capital story.

6 December

Cold raw morning, M J went to Todmorden by the train. Will and myself ran up after dinner in the car, we just dodged the rain, but all the hills were covered with snow, got back home 7:40.

7 December

Better today as regards weather. Mrs. Law sent us three tickets for "Greek Slave", Halifax Amateurs.

8 December

Accepted Mrs Laws kindly offer of tickets for the Greeks Slaves by the Halifax Light Opera Company (Royal) Amateurs, we met her there and we enjoyed the piece very much.

9 December

Dull, foggy day. Still upset at the mill, hands had to deal with somebody "chucking" every day. Bought 1 lb of Danish butter today 1/5d, next week will see it more. Fish is prohibitive, common Hake 5/- per stone.

10 December

Great naval victory, the Pacific disaster avenged. Three German cruisers and two colliers sunk.

The Pacific disaster refers to the naval Battle of Coronel on 1st November when a superior German force decisively defeated the British, sinking two of their four ships with no losses to themselves. Revenge came on 8th December when British reinforcements sank three of the five German ships at the Falkland Islands.

11 December

Wilf Hoyle left today. Turkey commits suicide.

The reference to Turkey's suicide presumably is a belated reference to her joining the war on the German's side on 29th October.

12 December

Finished another hard week.

13 December

Dull day. Will ran his mother up to Mrs Rothwell's in the afternoon. I walked up in the evening.

14 December

Heavy dull day. No very important news today but I think the tide is turning, we seem to be wearing them down, all the enemy's attacks are repulsed with heavy losses and we gradually gain ground.

15 December

Splendid day for a change, sunshine.

16 December

German raid in the north sea. Four cruisers appear off the east coast. Scarborough, Whitby and Hartlepool shelled, great damage done to property and many lives lost, the country now becoming alarmed but it's only bluff, to destroy property and kill women and children, this is German Kulture it will stimulate us all the more. Russians resist desperate foe. Dull wet miserable cold day.

The German raid on the East coast was an attempt to draw the British fleet into a trap. 137 civilians were killed and 592 injured. The attack on defenceless civilians caused outrage in Britain and around the world as can be seen by William's diary.

17 December

Mr Cash of Halifax died today. The scientific world will lose a diligent student. Geology etc and all branches of natural history, I knew him very well, he was formerly cashier of the Union Bank Halifax.

18 December

Butter this week 1/6d per pound, highest price on record.

19 December

Halifax afternoon, snow and sleet, shop full of Christmas goods, we should be thankful, one would think there was no war going on. After tea went to Huddersfield with Will, went to the Palace never saw such trash put on a stage in my life it was ------ the place was packed, poor feebleminded folk.

20 December

Will took his mother to Todmorden in the afternoon, rather cold ride. Had tea ready for them, I cooked a wild duck which we all appreciated.

21 December

Some Belgian refugees have come to Greetland, they are housed at Gatehead close to the mill, Messrs Waller brothers have put the houses at their disposal.

22 December

French have ordered a forward move, this looks like a waning on the enemy's part, a wearing down policy will now start, then Kitchener will run all our forces in spring and finally end this Potsdam devil.

23 December

Maud sent Will "Jacob's Light Freights". A capital book for dull hours.

24 December

Paper tonight records the death of Ben Noble, West Vale used to come to my old friend Cassius Hanson, a man of literary tastes, and used to read to us while C worked. Ordered a new cheesing frame, we cannot go on any longer, it will be costly but it's the inevitable.

25 December

We cannot be merry this Christmas, we stayed at home. Received a few cards from old friends etc and the rest of the day was spent reading etc etc.

26 December

Dull day. Frank Buckley, Will's friend came to spend the weekend he is now 2nd Lieut in the Royal Army Service Corps, he is at present at Stirling, he looks very smart and full of enthusiasm to get to the front.

27 December

Fine morning but turned out wet the rest of the day, Frank left this morning for Leeds en route for Stirling with all our best wishes.

28 December

No particular war news today. Busy day at the mill, shorthanded, everybody is in the same position, young men joined the colours others started working in the woollen mills making khaki for the troops, they are giving good wages for novices but it must be got out.

29 & 30 December

Cotton trade is getting plenty of orders in heavy counts for the Government requirements but fine spinners are suffering very much. Burnley according to the papers is in a very bad way, almost all mills stopped or working a few days per week.

31 December

This closes 1914 which will be remembered through countless years, we are the victims not the authors of this cruel wicked war, but we are only defending human liberty and we shall get our reward. For ourselves it has been a very trying year in business many things have gone wrong and have caused money lost and no chance of making it good when profits are cut almost nil but thank God we have pulled through the storm which at times looked threatening, we have been given strength and had good health all of us and for this we must be thankful, as dear friend Dr Jowett says count your blessings.

<u>Good Story</u>

Two women had been to see their husbands off en route for the front, one said to the other, at the last I couldn't tell what to say to him so I said well so long old chap and if tha thumps Kaiser as thas thumped me he'll be sorry thas ever come.

1915

By the beginning of the year all sides were plotting their strategies. For the French the issue was quite straightforward. The Germans were occupying a significant part of northern France and needed to be ejected immediately and they planned a series of offensives to achieve that objective. The British were forced to adopt a subsidiary role as their army was too small to mount a decisive offensive of its own. They could only play a supporting role and mounted minor attacks at Neuve Chappelle and Loos while the French attacked in force in Artois and Champagne. None of these efforts were successful and the problems associated with attacking heavily fortified positions defended by resolute troops with machine guns and heavy artillery became apparent.

The British attacks showed some serious shortcomings, including the leadership, of the commander-in-chief Sir John French and this, together with his leak of confidential information to the press, led to his replacement by Sir Douglas Haig.

The apparent stalemate on the Western Front did not suit the First Lord of the Admiralty, Winston Churchill. Never a man to rest on his laurels, and always a gambler, he proposed an attack in the Mediterranean against Turkey at the Dardanelles to force open a sea route to Russia and knock the Turks out of the war. The army was lukewarm to the idea and declined to provide any troops for the landings which would be needed. Undeterred, Churchill sent a purely naval force which eventually led to troops being sent and landings made on the Turkish mainland. It resulted in the same stalemate as on the Western Front but under worse conditions and logistical difficulties with the troops being on the end of a long sea supply route.

The Germans on the other hand decided to go to the defensive on the Western Front and concentrate the bulk of their forces in the east in an effort to knock Russia out of the war. The Eastern Front was so big that it was not possible to build a continuous series of fortifications and the Germans with their superior tactics and troops and supported by their Austro-Hungarian allies, were able to achieve a series of victories and drive the Russians back. It was only the vastness of their country and the huge numbers of troops they were able to deploy that saved the Russians from complete defeat. Germany did however make one contribution to the Western Front. They decided to test a new weapon, poison gas, against the French troops in the Ypres Salient. The initial attack was a resounding success completely routing the panicked French troops and tearing a large gap in the Allied lines. Fortunately the Germans did not have the reserves available to exploit their success and the attack petered out, but a new and terrible dimension had been added to the war.

To fight this great European war, the newly appointed Secretary of State for War, Lord Kitchener, quickly realised that the British had to raise a new citizen army. He was hampered by the fact that, alone amongst the great European powers, the United Kingdom did not have conscription and therefore did not have a huge reserve of trained manpower to draw upon. To make matters worse it was politically difficult to introduce conscription and men had to be recruited on a voluntary basis. Initially in 1914 the response was good but by the spring of 1915 the volunteers were drying up and other measures needed to be tried.

The first thing the government did was to hold a census to find out how many men were available, which revealed that there were a surprising number of military age who had not yet volunteered, 5,000,000 of them in fact. Following this revelation the Group Scheme of Enlistment was introduced. It became popularly known as the Derby Scheme named after the man who was in charge, Lord Derby. The scheme was still voluntary and asked men to volunteer when they would be classed as being in the army but would not be immediately called up. Instead they would be placed in a group based on their age and marital status and would be called up in order, with the youngest unmarried men being called first. The scheme was not a success as it was unpopular with unmarried men. It became clear by the end of the year that more decisive action needed to be taken.

1 January

No person ever regarded the first of January with indifference – Charles Lamb

It may not be a happy one, but we can all wish one another a Brighter Year. This country of ours is passing thru the crisis of her existence. The year starts with the loss of the Battleship "Formidable" in the Channel, purported to have been sunk by mine.

2 January

Furious fighting around Argonne six assaults repelled by the French. M J went to see Miss Greenwoods Hipperholme.

3 January

Rain. Dull, dark wet day. This being the day appointed for Intercession on behalf of the Nation and Empire in this time of war I went to Evening service at St Johns West Vale. The service was very impressive, owing to the heavy wet rainfall the Church was not filled.

4 January

Rain. Today's news the fighting round Steinbach by the French has been very severe, but foot by foot they advanced.

5 January

Rain. Irving Holt who was playmates with Will and Arnold came to see us tonight. He joined the colours at the outbreak of the War and has been in training ever since. It has made a man of him, he goes to the front next month. It was most interesting to hear what he has had to do but he is sure he has done the right thing.

6 January

Tonight I went to the Pictures. Scenes from the seat of War. Actual camera pictures of Antwerp, Louvain etc etc, it was dreadful to look at showing the effects of shells, buildings falling etc and huge factories on fire, the wreck and devastation was something terrible to look at, it made one shiver, to think in the 20th Century we have such barbarous monsters as these Germans whose brutality knows no end. But thank God the time will come when they will get wiped off the map of Europe.

Joe Noble came on in the evening. Russians with their mighty army are making Eastern Prussia flee, half millions are said to be fleeing out of the country. Everybody has been anxious on opening of Parliament about bringing in Conscription. Lord Kitchener made no reference to it he said men were flocking to the colour nothing more, this man parries with no party, but does what he thinks for the best and England today should be thankful that we have a soldier like him at the crisis in our history.

Austria on their last legs.

7 January

Frank Buckley called to bid us good bye, he came from Stirling & was on his way home to Windsor. He did not stay long. He was full of enthusiasm. He goes to France in a few days. He is a very smart soldier and our best wishes for his welfare go with him. M J not so well these anxious times worry her very much.

8 January

Rain again today. We have had nothing else for weeks but soaking rain. Floods in many parts of the country. Mrs Eastwood and Hilda came on this afternoon and stayed till evening.

9 January

Dull day. Prices of provisions going up, flour, butter, in fact everything. Went to see Mr Sam Briggs glad to find him better.

10 January

Dull heavy day with rain evening. War news today, heavy fighting in the trenches, but the enemy are gradually driven back, bad weather for the poor tommies.

11 January

Rather better weather today. We were all tired tonight. The work we have in at present does very badly, it tries the hands very much and makes them difficult to manage.

12 January

Brighter day, daylight beginning to show, this will be some comfort to us. This horrid war still goes on, other nations are likely to be drawn in, Roumania, Greece and Italy, they will be allies but territory will be a gaining factor with them I expect.

13 January

Submarines seen close to Dover Harbour but they got back without being hit. A fleet of aircraft came over the other day but did no damage.

Rain. Harassing day for all of us, this heavy work will sure peg some of us out. Will takes it too much to heart, I am much concerned about him.

14 January

Rain. Will went to Rochdale on business. M J went with him for company, it was an unfortunate journey. The party he went to see was away, and to end all, the bike went wrong and they had to leave it there, turned out a wild wet night.

15 January

More terrible news today – Devasted Italy. Earthquake havoc, 18 towns wrecked, 20,000 dead, a large region of country round Rome has been destroyed. Dreadful rainy weather tonight, a regular soaker.

The earthquake occurred near to the city of L'Aquila and resulted in 30,000 deaths. Because of the war, the Italian Government chose not to ask for international assistance.

16 January

Will had a letter from Frank he had landed at Havre.

17 January

Will went with Craven to Rochdale on their machine to fetch it back. M J and myself went to Todmorden by the 12 train. Had dinner at Harley Villas. Afternoon we all went to moorland.

18 January

Will's 21st Birthday. Many Happy Returns of the day.

Owing to the great depression and not a fitting time to make merry, we postponed asking a few friends to honour it to another time. However, Mrs Eastwood, Hilda and George (Mr & Mrs Norminton) came along in the evening and had supper with us. (Aunty Jennie) Mrs Eastwood, gave him a beautiful silver cigarette case. Hilda and George pair of slippers, Aunty Bertha and Flora and John ebony walking stick, (Maud) Mrs Sutcliffe cigarette case. Mr and Mrs Owen Street cigarette case with monogram, some of these he will get exchanged for something else. Zeppelin raid on Yarmouth. 8:30 tonight a Zeppelin flew over Yarmouth and dropped bombs. 2 or 3 killed and property damaged.

20 January

Halifax and District this week are compelled by the Authorities to close all Public Houses and Clubs at 9 o'clock.

Regulations introduced under the Defence of the Realm Act (DORA) restricted the hours pubs could open between 12 noon-3:00pm and 6:30pm - 9:00pm. It was believed that soldiers and munitions workers were drinking too much and it was affecting their performance at work.

21 January

Wheat advanced to 54/- per quarter, highest price for 47 years. Cotton has risen over 1d per lb in a months time, this I am afraid will have a deterrent effect on the trade.

22 January

Sprinkling of snow first thing this morning but it soon disappeared. 30th Anniversary of our Wedding Day. Poor Turkey lost her country through listening to the Berlin Butcher.

23 January

We went to Mrs Rothwells in the evening, stayed supper.

25 January

The paper this morning brings the news of a Naval Battle in the North Sea. The German ships were coming for another raid on our coast but are trapped by our fleet under Sir David Beatty on the Lion, when they saw our fleet they turned back but they were chased and the fine speed of the Lion soon got within range and fired at the Blucher and soon had her crippled and in two hours she sank. The other ship would have fared badly but we dare not follow them as we were approaching the mined zone.

SIR DAVID BEATTY

27 January

Cold, dull foggy day. Kaisers Birthday 56. Rather a bad day, failure at La Bassee. Loss of a Zeppelin at Litan and torpedoing of a Cruiser in the Baltic.

Great dearth of work people, Lancashire in the cotton centres are short of little hands (piecers), the same applies here. Owing to the limit age imposed by the Education fools our trade will diminish because children are too old before they begin to do some work and are not capable of picking up their work they are taught now not to work.

Germans have lost 20,000 the last 3 days.

28 January

M Jane not so well. The Russians are making great progress. They have now got into Germany, have taken more prisoners than they can tell what to do with. Germany now will be hard pressed E & W and the end, although a long time yet, cannot be but one end and the end of German Militarism.

29 January

Tonight there was one of the most beautiful moonlight effects I ever saw. The moon was almost full and the clouds looked just like plains of snow, the colour was lovely.

30 January

New Cheese Winding Frame came. Very hard day, felt done up when finished getting it in. Am compelled to put in a Cheese Frame to do away with many piecers because we cannot get them, education demands them more than commercial interest. We can train cheese winders, for no skill is required, but to train a piecer is something difficult in these days. M J went to Halifax.

31 January

Dull day. German waiters occupation gone.

1 February

German submarine in the Irish Sea sank 3 vessels, one just outside the Mersey Bar. Two fitters came to put up the Winding Frame.

2 February

Wet day. Very busy day. Tonight we were alarmed, the fire alarm went about 9 o'clock. Geo Lumbs' Scatch Room on fire but it was not serious.

3 February

Busy day with having the fitters here, they have done very well, but they want all attention.

Vicar: You know Thomas you set the young men of the parish a bad example by going into public houses on Sunday. Why don't you take your own gallon of beer home on a night?

Thomas: Ah, Sir I couldn't gang t'sleep wi a gallon o beer in the house.

4 February

Stopped on one twiner today. Fitters finished the Winding Frame today. I am thankful they have taken all our attention, and with all our heavy work just now it has been hard on us at home, goodness only knows, life like this is awful.

Miss Braddon the popular Novelist died today, she has been devoted to literary work since 1860. She could claim the distinction of being the most-read lady novelist of her age "Lady Audley Secret" brought her first fame, her books are too numerous to mention, but I have read a great many and I have a great respect for her works, they have delighted one in the happy past and much better than some of the novels of the present day.

Recruiting in the neighbourhood going on very well, all the young fellows will be off in a very short time.

From this and other entries it can be seen that William was obviously proud that so many men were volunteering, but he saw no contradiction in the fact that his own son had not done so. The absence of any mention of this in the diary suggests that it was never really considered. This was quite normal. Although much is made of the 1.2 million men who by this time had volunteered, the majority of men of military age had not done so, some 5 million of them. This reluctance to come forward eventually led to the introduction of conscription.

6 February

Working late at mill getting fixed up with the frame etc etc. I intended going to Huddersfield to see "Carmen" but the exertion was too much so Will went by himself. He enjoyed it very much.

7 February

Bitter cold morning. Rain towards night. Will went to St John Choir Festival with his Mother. I could not go I had a bad attack of toothache.

8 February

Total British Casualties 104,000 to date. Of course this includes killed, wounded and missing.

9 February

Fire broke out at Pendleton Mills in Sid Thornton's room this morning. The room was soon in flames, the fire engine was soon on the scene and with hydrants they got it under, but not before it got into the room above, great damage was done with water. This mill was on fire last Oct 12 months and have only just got fairly going, it is a great pity. G Hancocks came to put one of our twiners on to bobbins.

10 February

The Premier Mr Asquith did a public service to the country this week Bill Muggins, Sam Suet, Tom Twist and other £400 year mugs wanted Parliament to go on passing their pet Bills etc. but he told them in clogmaster words no politics at a time of national peril. Other things far above these demand our attention.

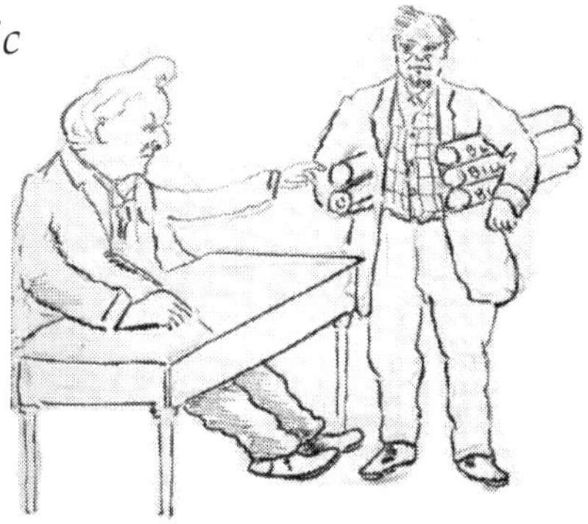

11 February

Kaiser calls a hasty War Council. His army's critical situation 45,000 Germans killed in East Poland costly effort to reach Warsaw.

13 February

The first sod of a new School "St Thomas" was cut at Greetland by Dr Jowett of Coley, a worse day could scarcely be imagined, the snowfall being continuous and the ground a foot deep in slush. I had a difficulty in getting there, to brave the elements, was a labour of love for the old place. Dr Jowett preached a capital sermon. "It is not the will of your Father which is in heaven that one of these little ones should perish." Tea was provided in the old school. Dr Jowett told some good stories of old Sam Jagger etc.

This is a scene of the start of work on the Sunday School building at St Thomas Church, Greetland, Halifax. The building is still used by the church and other groups today.

I came down to Shrove Tide Tea Party. They had a capital entertainment etc. a number of Belgian Refugees were invited. West Vale Church in the evening. Dr Jowett came to take duty for Mr Richardson. He came back with us for supper, tho night was very cold and he had had a very heavy day we persuaded him to stay all night, we were pleased to have his company.

The popular song "Kathleen Mavourneen" was composed by F N Crouch – words by Julia Crawford an Irishwoman. D'Almaine the publisher is said to have made £15,000 by the song, though Crouch only £10 for the copyright.

Frederick Crouch (1808-1896) was a musician and composer born in London who emigrated to America in 1849 where he fought for the Confederacy during the American Civil War. The song "Kathleen Mavourneen" was very popular at the time and features frequently in the musical score of the 1993 film "Gettysburg".

15 February

Dr Jowett left us for home 9.30 am.

16 February

Better day. Pancakes this year I am afraid will not be as plentiful as usual, eggs 1½d and flour 2/11d per stone. Strange customs still survive. Girls I noticed today playing shuttlecock and the boys spinning tops and playing marbles.

17 February

Dull heavy day, shorthanded at mill, had to sack a weary Willie yesterday, and tonight another sends word he cannot come tomorrow, expect Lloyd George will claim him for a week or so. This business now is not worth the candle if we did not all work like niggers we should be ruined in 3 months, hands will not work now. Railway Co are curtailing trains, ½ day tickets, workmen's tickets etc, and all Excursions at Easter and Whitsuntide, serves the public right if the Trade Unions have forced this on the Railway Co they must suffer by it.

Lord Normanby, when Master of Mulgrave School Whitby was written to by a father who wished his boy to be educated there and added I'm told you take only the sons of gentlemen. "If your boy" the master wrote back "behaves well, nobody will ask who his father is".

18 February

Today was fixed by the Kaiser when he was going to wipe us off the map of Europe, but it has not come off. The Government are now going to stop all food stuffs etc going into Germany even through neutral countries, so we shall now bring another ally into force "Starvation".

19 February

Cold, damp uncomfortable day. Have been running machinery until 8 o'clock since and we all feel dished, with being shorthanded.

20 February

Merchants Ships sunk in the Irish Sea by German Submarines, this is getting too near to be pleasant. Cold raw day, helped Will to get the Motor Cycle fit for the coming weather.

21 February

Will took his Mother to Todmorden but it turned out unfavourable, but they managed to get home between the heavy rain but it was a cold ride.

22 February

Depressing reports from the Front. Russians have been driven back. Cargo boats sunk in the Channel by submarines. Working until 8 o'clock.

23 February

Hard day at the mill, everything gone wrong today. Busy putting up crane.

Mr J R Smith

This gentleman many years ago issued drawings of all the well known Streets in Halifax, the public buildings and old houses, as they were 70 or 80 years ago. They were very interesting and they were afterwards copied on postcards and I have about 1 doz. of them. He was an Architect and was in some way connected with the Halifax Corporation.

24 February

A repetition of yesterday's doings at the mill, it never rains but it pours.

Bombardment of the Dardanelles by the English and French Fleet. If this can be successfully accomplished it will free Russia for her fleet and release her of her wealth of corn for the world.

25 February

Cold frosty weather. War news still very gloomy.

26 February

Cold North wind. Strike threatening all over the country on account of the war owing to risks etc food stuffs are going up, and now the Trade Unions are agitating for higher wages. What will be the outcome, I see nothing but civil war as they have got master of the situation.

27 February

Man cannot live without some change in all this worry, so I went to Halifax to a "Matinee" Cavaliere F. Castellano Co in the "Lily of Killarney" a capable Co and I enjoyed it.

Went up to see Mrs Eastwood at West Royd. Turned out a most miserable night, rain and snow. Will went to Oldham to spend the weekend.

Sarah Bernhardt the Great French Actress sorry to hear to have to undergo operation of leg amputation, the world will sympathise with actress, her death scene I shall ever remember, so realistic.

28 February

Cold raw day. We felt very lonely without Will but I got all my accounts out for the month etc. Will came home about 9 o'clock.

<u>Sarah Bernhardt.</u> the Great French Actress sorry to hear she have to undergo operation of leg amputation the world will sympathize with her, I saw her play at Leeds a very long time ago. She was a wonderful actress, her death scene I shall ever remember so realistic

1 March

Fleet's havoc at the Dardanelles the straits are now free for 7½ miles. Russians still making progress.

2 March

Showery and very cold. Sorry to see in the paper the death of F J Bullen, the well known writer. If you want a whiff of the briney read his books. I cherish one of his books the "Grave of the Cachalof" but all his works are good, not a bad one, he put many old notions etc about Whales aside showing some nationalists were off their horse and were told by them that the whale lived on small fry of the ocean, but he tell us differently in the "Grave of the Cachalof". All his books are written by a most keen observer of nature, and a deep religious tone pervades all his books. I consider him the best writer of the era. I have read after and I have read a few.

Frank Bullen (1857-1915) was born into poor circumstances and went to sea at the age of 12. He later wrote a number of books and articles about his experiences.

3 March

Still working until 8 o'clock. All work, the talk is nothing else but work. Thank God we have had pleasure in the past, this is the only consolation just now.

Making progress at the Dardanelles only 2 or 3 forts now remain. This will be the final scene of the Turkish Empire.

4 March

All the lamps with exception of one at the street end are extinguished on account of the fear of German aircraft coming. It looks very gloomy at night now, but we had to do without formerly.

5 March

German submarine sunk in the Channel. Blockade of all ships now going to Germany so we are getting nearer the end, we shall practically starve them out.

"When the bough break the burden will fall, down will come Turkey & sausage and all."

6 March

Raw day. Will took his Mother to Greetland with flowers for Arnold. I called to see Mr Briggs (Sam) glad to see him better, think he will clog again with the coming of the Cuckoo. Dr Potts called today.

7 March

Beautiful sunny morning. Heard a mistle thrush singing up in the wood, this foretells spring. Came in dull afternoon and threatened rain.

8 March

Government bringing in a Bill to take over any Factory or Workshop necessary for the making of any war material. Reading Dumas "Black Tulip" splendid, when I have time.

9 March

Better day. The Germans torpedoed three English Boats today, and the English rammed one of their Submarines and captured their crews.

10 March

English and French Fleet are still pegging away in the Dardanelles and doing heavy damages to the Forts. German submarines still keep torpedoing our merchant ships, one off Scarbro, one off Fleetwood and one in South Wales.

11 March

Very busy today, have more work offered than I can do, still we are working until 8 o'clock.

12 March

Mrs Eastwood came on this evening. M J had some interesting tit bits for her.

13 March

Bright day. Harvey & Frank came from Oldham to spend the weekend with us. Will took them to Huddersfield. I went to see Joe Noble who was laid up with Bronchitis, but glad to find him improving, he was still confined to his bed.

14 March

The boys ran up to Greetland with flowers for Arnold. Will took Harvey and Frank to Todmorden on the machine. M J followed on by train.

15 March

M Jane Uncle (Thomas Ashworth) died today at Urmston near Manchester, the last male line of the Ashworth family of 10 children. War news this morning talks of heavy fighting, but still making progress. Submarines are doing dreadful work in sinking poor unarmed boats in different parts of the coast.

16 March

At last the Dresden the German warship was sunk in the Pacific close to "Juan Fernandes" or Robinson Crusoe Island. This ship has done much damage in the western waters, there are only 2 more raiders on the high seas.

The SMS *Dresden* was the sole German survivor from the Battle of the Falkands in December 1914. She was finally trapped in Chilean waters where British ships violated Chilean neutrality to sink her.

17 March

Lord Kitchener made a memorable speech in the house about the shirkers and the slackers.

Herbert Speak, I see was buried today at the pretty little Church of Heysham.

Tonight records the death of Mr I Ingham Learoyd of Halifax. He was born at Ripponden, he was partner in Pickard Learoyd & Co Accountants. He was a man of many parts. 30 years ago he used to come to West Vale, he was a clever conjurer, he did the box trick, handcuff etc. and a clever card manipulator, he was well known amateur photographer, and for 30 years travelled the continent and then gave lantern lectures in the winter. I have

heard him many times, he crossed the North Sea 88 times. He left £4,000 odd.

18 March

Cold morning but towards night we had the heaviest snowstorm we have had for a long time, a regular blizzard. Terrible railway accident at Smithy Bridge many killed and injured.

19 March

Bad in the streets first thing but towards noon thaw set in. Another Wage Day, we dread them coming round, higher wages and less production and hand leaving or something, it is not worth the candle.

20 March

Halifax with M J we gave ourselves an intellectual treat we went to Mattins of Edward Compton Co in "Sir Rodger de Coverley" a new piece to Halifax, and in the Evening we went to see him in Davy Garrick.

Notes

"Sir Rodger de Coverley" was played exceedingly well, every character well portrayed, the setting was splendid and we both enjoyed it. M J particularly, so much so that we went in the evening to see him in Davy Garrick which of course needs no praise of mine. Edward Compton is a player of sterling worth, and one I have seen times with number. He made a short speech at the close, and thanked those who had payed him a visit, he said he might never come again. Edward Compton the well known actor with his Company are at Halifax this week in a round of good sterling plays, but I see as usual with the present day patrons, they are playing to empty houses. Next week with a Musical Comedy, with trashy music, and vulgar patter the place will be packed.

Edward Compton (1854-1918) was a well known actor of Shakesperian comedies. His son was Compton Mackenzie the author of "Whiskey Galore".

Scene in Davy Garrick Chambers

His daughter Miss Constance Pelissier played leading parts with him.

21 March

Bright morning for the 1st of Spring. Our wishes are that everything was as bright. M J and Will had a run over Cockhill to Todmorden.

22 March

Russians coup. Fall of Przmsyl, 9 Generals and 117,000 men surrender.

Przemsyl was a fortress city in Galicia (now Poland) which had been under siege by the Russians since October 1914. It was back in Austrian hands by June 1915.

23 March

Every commodity going up. Coals and all food stuffs are gradually going up, we are in for a bad time. It's about time the working man should feel his feet. I don't care how he suffers, because they have all got so lazy to earn their living.

24 March

Beautiful day.

Lady Visitor: That's a bad case, what are you going to do with him

Orderly: Oh e's going back to the front.

Lady Visitor: Good heavens what for

Orderly: E thinks e knows who done it.

London Opinion

Conscription talked about very freely and it looks very likely, things are beginning to look black. I should not like our boy to be pressed in, in fact we could not do anything without him.

25 March

Submarines busy again in the Channel, more steamers sunk, this sort of warfare I am afraid will do us a great deal of harm, our mercantile boats are found to suffer, this something we little dreamed of.

26 March

Another pay day over, this is a day we all dread, somebody always grumbling etc etc, everybody who employ labour all tell the same story, more wages and less production.

27 March

Bitter cold day. Went with Will to Holmfirth then over the hill 1212ft to Durford Bridge, splendid view of the moor and hills, came back by Honley, but the cold wind was cruel and we had road troubles to make matters worse.

Baden Powell the originator of the Boy Scouts, no wonder he has the natural instinct of scouting, seeing he is a descendent of the Red Skins, thru Princess Pocahontas, "La Belle Sauvage" who died and was buried at Gravesend. Having saved the life of one Englishman Capt John Smith from the savage fury of her father, she afterwards married another John Rolfe to whom she bore a son from whom BP is descended you can see it on her face, if you look at his profile.

We can find no mention anywhere else of a connection between Pocahontas and Baden Powell, one must wonder where William found this nugget of information.

28 March

Got up late. Owen and Mrs Winterbottom came in just at dinner time, they had motored over. They left in the afternoon M J and Will went part of the way home with them.

Just as we were going to bed Dr Potts drop in, we had a long sitting.

29 March

I believe they will close Public Houses more than they are at present, people cannot afford to spend on drink just now and besides that drink won't work.

30 March

Very bitter cold, wind all day. Felt very tired somehow today. Working until 8 o'clock. Shorthanded as we are is too much

31 March

More British ships torpedoed by submarines, this piratical method is downright murder, they sink Trawlers, colliers, etc then laugh as they see the poor defenceless sailors drowning. Total Abolition is talked about, Public Houses closed at 9 o'clock, this will bring some people to sober thinking that we are passing thru one of the greatest epochs of the World.

1 April

This the 1st of April and got thru without being made a fool, perhaps in these strained times people have not time. No lamps lit at night, and all shops and Mills ordered to keep down excessive lighting.

2 April

We had no Cross Buns today, not missed for a long long time. <u>Rent Day</u> Owing to the rise in coal of 3/5d per ton they have put up our rent £20 per annum. This will be heavy for us, unless we can get our prices up, which is terrible hard work.

3 April

Damp cold raw day, poor prospects for Easter. No one will appreciate the Holiday more than we shall at home, for our work of late has been heavy and we all have worked like niggers. Sorry to hear that my old friend Joe Noble, who has just recovered from a severe attack of Bronchitis has accidentally fallen down the stairs and broken two ribs, not so serious I heard afterwards. Trouble never came alone it seems. I hope he will be alright in a few weeks.

4 April

Very cold and a gale blowing. I went with Will in the sidecar to see Bertha. Glad to say found her better but it has pulled her down, got home alright but it was a cold journey.

Annual Meeting of the 'Henpect' Club at Sowerby, the account in the evening paper is very humorous.

The Hen Pecked club was a humorous male social club which met annually on Easter Monday, alleged to be the only day of the year that they had any degree of freedom from their wives.

5 April

Bright day but threatening. I stayed at home and had a rest, I had a good novel and I was very happy. M J and Will ran down to Dewsbury. Called to see Mr and Mrs Maitchell (Charlotte) They were pleased to see them. M J taken very badly in the evening.

6 April

Wet cold uncomfortable day. M J in bed part of the day but feels very weak, with the straining of last night's sickness. We all stayed at home today.

The previous entries demonstrate that the war was hitting. Before the war there was almost no state interference in people's lives but the introduction of restricted opening hours for licensed premises, restrictions on the times lights could be lit and requisitioning of goods and premises for the war effort were only the start of numerous regulations that pervaded people's everyday lives.

7 April

M J still very weak. Will also got a severe cold in his head. Started work again today and for a wonder all turned up.

An Inn Sign

The Hanging Gate

This gate hangs free
And hinders none
Refresh yourselves
And travel on

There is no "We'll just have another and then ……."

Rates and Taxes all going up with leaps and bounds, we are in for trying times.

8 April

Cold raw damp weather. Yorkshire Regiments have suffered heavy losses, both in officers and men in the last great battle Neuve Chapelle.

9 April

Several boats have been lost this last few days with submarines, crews given but a few moments to leave their ships then blown up.

10 April

Beautiful day. Went to Halifax in the evening to get my hair cut, the town looked very strange. Streets poorly lit and all shops had lowered lights. M J came up to meet me. We intended going to the pictures "Little Minister" but it was crowded so we came home.

11 April

Dull cold day.

12 April

Great move of troops from England now taking place. John Bull will I hope come up to his usual expectation.

13 April

Tonight in the House the Premier announced that up to the present we have lost 140,000, this is terrible to think of the pick of the nation.

14 April

Zeppelin raid tonight at Blythe bombs were dropped, but glad to say not much damage done. At Halifax tonight about 10 o'clock all the trams were stopped and all electricity turned off. Places of amusement had to close this is coming to close quarters. No special war news today. Italy are wavering, they would like to join the Allies, but up to now are undecided.

A Zeppelin raid by a single craft on 14th April on the Northumberland and Tyneside areas caused little damage, but chaos reigned in Halifax. Although the incident was over 100 miles away the authorities turned off the electric current extinguishing all electric lamps and halting the trams. Places of entertainment were phoned and told to evacuate their premises and the fire alarm buzzers at two local mills were sounded which had the opposite effect of what was intended as people came into the streets to see where the fire was. This included the local Fire Brigade who were called by concerned citizens. Of course nobody had thought to inform the population that the buzzers were also doubling up as an air raid warning!

15 April

Some of our Territorials Halifax and district who have been in training since last August are off to the Front, we have many friends amongst them, our best wishes go with them.

The local Territorials were the 4th Battalion West Riding Regiment who arrived in France on 14th April. They served with distinction on the Western front for the remainder of the war.

16 April

Another visit today Zeppelins came across to Kent but did little damage.

17 April

Ted Buckley came to spend the weekend with Will. M J and myself went to Halifax to see (Miss Dorothy West Symes) in "A Soldier and a Man" but we did not care for the play rather seen her in a good comedy.

Britain's New Problem

Wave of Emotional Nonsense "about the unmarried Mother". The problem of the large number of unmarried girls and women in this country who are expecting to become Mothers is been discussed in all the papers and pulpits throughout the country but not as a rule wisely. No one wants to make out and apportion blame in this matter, but it is an even mistake to begin to glorify human frailty as though it were praiseworthy, the state has enough on its shoulders, without having to bear this shameful cost as some people would have it.

M J got a maid of all work to come and help her to do the usual spring cleaning.

18 April

Owen and Harvey motored over this afternoon stayed tea. Will and Ted had gone to their house, so they returned early to catch our folks before they started back. I went on to spend an hour with Joe Noble he was still in bed but had been up a few hours.

20 April

War materials so the Premier tells us are putting out their fullest extent. We are even supplying our allies with some. More shot and shell were used around Neuve Chapelle than what we used in all the *<u>Boer War</u>.*

21 April

Ted went home this afternoon. I think he has enjoyed the weekend very much. Will took him to the station, he misses him very much they were such good pals. Heavy fighting again today, ground gained, heavy losses to the enemy. Italy still hesitates.

22 April

Cold day but fine. Time is precious now, to enter up my diary is a struggle, but to put the usual sketches in I am afraid is on the wane.

23 April

Will busy taking his Motor Engine down for sundry repairs so expect it will be a few days before we get running again.

24 April

Thus ends another trying week what with high wages and short handed the game now is not worth the candle. We are all sick and downhearted there seems no luck for us, the more we work the less we get.

25 April

West Vale in the evening to see Joe Noble he was still confined to his bedroom but better.

26 April

Germans are using poisonous gas bombs, which have been the cause of heavy losses. This dastardly act put them outside the pale of civilisation but they will resort to anything if it will gain a point of vantage.

The Germans used poison gas for the first time on 22nd April starting the 2nd Battle of Ypres. Not for the first time, they had crossed a moral line causing revulsion around the world and giving the Allied propagandists a field day.

27 April

Still heavy fighting in the Yser front. Some positions which we left have been regained with heavy losses to the enemy.

28 April

M J Birthday Many Happy Returns

Charles Trevelyan member for Elland Division has been kindly kicked out of the division by his own party. He is a pro German and spoken against the government for going to war, so when a man turns against his own country, he deserves something more than be kicked out, he is a Democratic Humbug of the deepest dye.

Sir Charles Trevelyan (1870-1958) was the Liberal MP for Elland and opposed Britain's entry into the war, resigning from the Government in protest to set up the Union of Democratic Control to rally opposition. William's opinion of him is quite clear and is probably influenced by Trevelyan's position in society. He was a member of the aristocracy with all the wealth and trappings that came with it, but was left wing in his views eventually joining the Labour Party and serving in their first ever cabinet in 1924. He could be described as a "Champagne" Socialist.

29 April

Busy all day, working like niggers, no time for rest when you get home you cannot have patience ever to read and I have such a lot of books to read and time going.

Lieut. George Taylor Ramsden married today at St Georges Church London to Miss Elizabeth Juel Hansen a Norwegian, he has contested Elland Division in two Elections in the Conservative interest. I think he will be returned next Election.

Good Luck

30 April

New Licensing Bill State control dearer Beer and weaker whisky, double duty on spirits. I think this is too much, as usual the moderate temperate man has to suffer for the drunken shirker. Of course wages have got so high that a man can afford to go on the spree for 2 or 3 days and then earn what will keep him. This Bill I suppose will perhaps be altered when the War is over. The present alterations are for increasing the output of munitions of War.

1 May

Will busy with his Motor Cycle putting in new crank shafts, a difficult job but with a little help has succeeded.

2 May

St Johns West Vale Anniversary. M J and myself went to the evening service. Vicar of Lightcliffe preached, Mr Eastwood, Hilda and George there.

3 May (Bank Holiday)

Naval actions in the North Sea. British destroyer torpedoed. Two German submarines were sunk. White frost early morning, this will be bad for the blossoms.

4 May

Today news not so rosy. The Russians are said to have suffered a severe reverse, we have had a severe fight again, and have had heavy losses, the Canadians suffered the worst.

5 May

The German submarines have again showed their gallant bravery by sinking 8 or 9 harmless Trawlers from Hull and Grimsby up to the present they have sunk about 54.

Coal 24/- a Ton

Owing to the war, the annual letting of pitches on Blackpool sands, which last year £2,700 was raised, could get no offers at all.

6 May

Warm day, splendid growing weather just now. In the evening we had a tour round Brighouse, Hipperholme and Halifax. The trees are pushing out their leaves and the fields looking very green.

7 May

The death took place this afternoon of Elland's oldest inhabitant Miss Lucy Hammerton of Westgate, she has been a great worker for the Church here, she has left a permanent record of Elland life in her book "Olde Elland" which will keep green a fragrant memory. I have the book it has one fault it is too short.

The mammoth Cunarder "Lusitania" was torpedoed this afternoon in broad daylight off the Irish Coast nearly 2000 souls on board. 703 up to date are said to be saved. This leaves the appalling loss 1275, many notable men were lost including A Vanderbilt the American Millionaire and C Frohman and many others. Germany seems more determined than ever to wade to world power thru blood of innocent millions. The loss of this ship deplorable as it is on many grounds, but the loss of life is enough to set the rest of the world ablaze with fury against the Teutonic race, this latest incident is an illustration of frightfulness carried to its highest or lowest degree.

The RMS *Lusitania* was torpedoed by a German submarine on 7th May leading to the loss of 1,195 lives including 128 Americans, a fact which enraged public opinion in the USA. The British claimed that the sinking was in contravention of the rules of war which at this time forbade the sinking of unarmed vessels without a warning. The Germans responded, with some justification, that the ship was carrying munitions (which she was) and was classed as an armed merchant cruiser. There was also a suspicion that the vessel was deliberately placed in harm's way to bring the USA into the war.

Controversy has raged ever since, fuelled by the refusal of the British government to release papers relating to the incident.

8 May

We are all dumfounded this morning at the loss of the "Lusitania" our nerves have been on the rack so long but this is a sad and terrible blow, could not read the paper this morning it was too much. Military Display at Huddersfield a detachment 16 Yorkshires marched thru Elland this afternoon.

9 May

Ma and Will went to Todmorden afternoon. Coming home they broke down at Tuel Lane, had to leave the car there and come home in a taxi. Landed here about 12 o'clock. I was in a terrible state.

10 May

Working overtime again this week. The greatest indignation from all parts of the world on the sinking of the Lusitania, American papers are wild but Almighty Dollar is too beloved by Jonathan to make a protest.

Jonathan is a slang term for the Americans.

11 May

Desperate battle for Calais. Fierce fighting on a 70 mile front, our losses lamentably heavy. Whole German battalions swept away.

12 May

Heavy rain last night but it will do the greatest possible good for our crops. Bitter cold day, rain and snow, the hills have a slight covering. Special Cabinet Meeting. The last act of the barbarous Germans has roused England. All Germans I believe, whether naturalised or not will be interned. On the Stock Exchange they have been forbidden to come on the boards.

13 May

H.M.S. Goliath sunk in the Dardanelles torpedoed over 500 lives lost. This is very depressing news, the strain is getting intolerable. All reports indicate that in Flanders and the N of France a great move forward on the part of the allies is in progress this means a decisive blow for the Germans.

Grasshopper Warbler heard in the Hebden Valley this is very rare so far north, I remember they said some 30 years ago there was one at Elland (Top Lock). I went with Cassius Hanson several nights but found it was the Reed Warbler, this bird is a beautiful singer and very imitative but sings most at night.

14 May

Bitter cutting E wind. Russians have reverses in Galicia.

Crusade against Aliens very bitter, shops wrecked and hundreds interned, they are only spies, so out they go.

The sinking of the RMS *Lusitania* provoked a surge of anti German feeling with serious incidents of looting against properties owned by people with German sounding names occurring across the country. There were no reported acts of overt hostility in the Halifax area.

15 May

Had a run on the moors to Buckstones this afternoon, very pleasant. Met Mr & Mrs Street they had come over Bill O Jack and are going home. Went to Dudwell with Joe Noble showed me a number of beautiful tombs they have erected there. Saw Mrs Oddy bringing her tribute of affection. On two sides of the grave are line sketches of the Reaper and the Stone Breaker, two of his well known pictures.

16 May

Fine clear day but rather cool. M J and Will ran over to Oldham in the morning.

17 May

This afternoon about 700 4th W.R.Reg under Col Land called at Elland, they are changing their camps, then they go abroad. It was a sorry sight to see such young blood, the pride of the country to be shot at like birds, but we are all proud of them to think they are fighting for home and country, and putting down forever these barbarian German Huns, I doff my hat to you lads & wish you safe return. Re-shuffling the Cabinet, members of the opposition (Tories) to be brought into the cabinet. This I consider the proper thing in a crisis like this we want the best men to fill these positions irrespective of their politics. Party politics are a hindrance to the nation at large that's my opinion.

Heard a very good story and true as well. Some lady living near our relations at Todmorden was reading in the paper about some of her friends who are fighting in the trenches been poisoned by the foul gases used by the Germans. Got very much excited and vowed she would go out and herself murder some of these dreadful Huns. Her little son aged 5 or 6 years began to cry and he said 'Don't Go Mamma let me go instead of you'. MH

War does harden our feeling we can <u>all say with Robert Burns</u>.

I wave the quantum o' the sin

The hazard o' concealing

But Och; it hardens a' within

And petrifies the feeling

19 May

Steady progress been made by the Allies. The Germans are been driven further back. Italy in revolt, but not definitely decided on going to war, but it coming for all that.

20 May

Dull day. Lord Kitchener asking for 300,000 more men to finish the War. We are now living in daily dread of Conscription, some papers are very persistent that it should come in.

21 May

Many well known Public Houses are compelled to close their doors. The recent restrictions have completely shut them out of making a decent living.

22 May

Stopped today for the Holidays and we all can do with them but in these times one refrains going in for any enjoyment.

Appalling disaster at "Gretna" troop train wrecked, three passenger trains burned, this disaster assumes a magnitude unknown in the United Kingdom. Up to now 158 dead and missing, 175 injured, one regiment the Royal Scotch suffered the most. It seems too horrible to describe, nothing left of the train but charred wreckage. These noble hearted lads off to fight for dear old England to be lost like this, is nothing less than a sad calamity.

The Gretna Green disaster happened on 22nd May when a troop train carrying the 1/7th Royal Scots collided with a local passenger train and they were then both hit by an express train to Glasgow. The wreckage caught fire with the loss of approximately 226 lives. The figure cannot be more exact as the records of the Royal Scots were lost in the blaze. A further 246 were injured. It remains the deadliest train crash in British history.

23 May – *Whit*

"Blands" Swan Hotel Grasmere. HOT. Will and myself started 9.30 this morning in beautiful weather to run to Ambleside, got there about 4.30. Dixons Restaurant. Slept Bells Apartment. We started along with Mr Dixon who was going to Grange. He has similar machine to ours, via Bradford, Keighley, Settle, Kirby Lonsdale, then on to Kendal, the country was delightful round here. We rode thru miles of blossom on each side of the road. Kendal is very interesting place, then on to Ambleside. The trees are just at their best and we lingered long on the road to admire. After tea and a good wash which we needed we ran on in the cool of the evening to Rydal Water, Grasmere. Here we stayed to pay homage to Wordsworth but looking at his grave, we were late off should have gone in to service but

loitered reverently outside. Then forward up the hill to the top with Thirlmere at our feet, then we came back same way and the mountains were rich in colour with the changing lights, which I cannot describe. Getting back we looked up a friend who lives here (Mr Dixon) who took us to a beautiful waterfall which was well worth the visit – a most excellent bed finished our days run.

24 May – *Whitsun - Bank Holiday*

Empire Day. HOT. Left Ambleside 9.30 ran to Bowness. Here it was delightful in the golden sunshine then to Kendall thru a beautiful county to Lancaster, then across country to Morecambe here we rested, then, thru the Fylde county to Blackpool, then home. Starting with a good breakfast in brilliant sunshine, we ran down to Bowness. Some parts very hilly but very pretty. We sat down here under the trees for the heat was intense and we were loth to leave such a beautiful picture, then on again to Kendal, down the N road to Milnthorpe and here I may say the best of roads I have ever been on, until we got to Lancaster. This city has a great attraction for me. John O Gaunts' Embattled Pile we could see a long way off. After leaving here we struck across country to Morecambe which was interesting. The Town was very busy indeed. We ran down the promenade and stayed a short time then forward across the Fylde Country, struck the river Wye and ran along its banks for a long way and in some parts very picturesque then thru Poulton to Blackpool. Had tea with Mrs Robinson, then made for Todmorden. M J was watching for us. This ends a most delightful 2 days holiday for which we must be thankful.

25 May

HOT. Beautiful day. Italy at last proclaims War on Germany and Austria.

In spite of her alliance with Austria and Germany, Italy declared war against them on 23rd May. The allies had successfully enticed the Italians with offers of Austrian territory. A new front was opened but with the same result as elsewhere, stalemate.

26 May

Very cold E wind. Quite a decided change from Sunday, Monday and Tuesday. A long time since we had such a glorious Whitsuntide.

27 May

Germans using their poisonous gases again, this is not warfare.

"There is no greater sorrow

Than to be mindful of the happy time in misery" *Bartlett*

28 May

H.M.S MAJESTIC torpedoed in the Dardanelles. Beefsteak today 1/6 per lb. Scores of butchers are compelled to close their shops.

29 May

Mrs Arthur Law laid the Foundation Stone St Thomas' School, sorry I could not get there.

30 May

Restful day. M J went to Evening Service St Johns'.

31 May

Zeppelin raid on London but not much damage, they came at night and are bad to locate. We are making progress at the Dardanelles, but is a tough struggle they are so well fortified.

After unsuccessful attempts by the British and French navies to force their way through the Dardanelles troops were landed on 25th April, but due to a combination of poor leadership and determined resistance by the Turks, little progress was made. The same problems that were found on the Western Front also dogged operations here. The senior allied military leaders simply considered the campaign as an unnecessary diversion of troops from the decisive front in France and Belgium.

1 June

Germans still bombarding Rheims Cathedral. What sacrilege. This will bring the contempt of the World against this inhuman monster.

2 June

Threatened Strike in the Cotton Trade. William Ashworth Stott served with a summons by the Ingleton Police for none production of license when asked for it.

Russians had a setback at the last moment they fell short of ammunition and had to retire. The Germans are simply raining shells this shows their preparedness.

3 June

Only a word command but it loses or wins the field.

Only a stroke of the pen, but a heart is broken or healed.

4 June

Wm. Ashworth Stott today at the Ingleton Court was fined 6/6 for not producing his license when asked for by Police Officer on the 5 inst.

5 June

M J very ill during the night and in fact up to noon today bad bilious attack. I could not go to the mill. Will ran up for Bertha, but she was much better when she got here.

Just finished reading the Channings one must block out this horrid war for the moment. I have read it with delight, a charming book, beautiful language and full of real Christian character. The Victorian age has no better writer than Mrs Hy Wood.

Mrs Henry Wood (1814–1887) was a popular Victorian writer and also editor of the magazine *Argosy* until it's closure in 1901. She was born Ellen Price in Worcestershire and wrote over thirty novels to support her family after the death of her husband in 1866.

6 June

M J better. Orson & Harvey called this afternoon but did not stay. Harvey is going in for a Commission, he can stand it no longer so he says.

7 June

Zeppelin raid again on the E Coast. 4 or 5 killed & 40 wounded. Still severe fighting. Gaining ground slowly. Very depressing to see every day casualties lists of some of our local men. It is terrible. One wonders how long this terrible horror can go on.

8 June

Constantinople is sad straights we shall soon be there. Hottest day this year 71.9° in the shade.

9 June

Anxiously waiting of American Note to Germany.

Up to now the War has cost us more than £800,000,000 or 3 Million a day just for one moment think of what untold misery this will bring on children yet unborn.

The party who plotted against Lord Kitchener are now trying to get Mr Asquith out of office, but their puny efforts will fail.

We as a Nation are now a proud hen that Munition shops all over the country and putting their best efforts to bring out more shells.

Our losses up to the end of last month was 258,000. This is appalling but sad as it is, we must fight it thru, if we are not to be trodden under the tyrannical feet of the Germans whose sole religion is power and that by any means, they are taught that from childhood.

The note was a protest by the American Government about the sinking of the RMS *Lusitania*. The USA did not enter the war at this time but unrestricted submarine warfare was ended in September by the Germans.

The references to plots are about the "Shell Scandal" in the Spring of 1915 when the Commander of the BEF, Sir John French, blamed the shortage of shells for the failure of his attacks. The Liberal PM, Asquith, was forced to form a coalition government and set up the Ministry of Munitions.

10 June

Many British ships torpedoed this week, this warfare is causing heavy losses to the Nation.

11 June

Very warm day. Lloyd George great appeal to workpeople for greater unity and put ammunition etc. etc. on the front rank. It by this alone can the War be brought to a successful and speedy ending.

12 June

Walked up to Greetland with M J with flowers for Arnold. The moss on the grave was full of <u>*blossom*</u> *and looked very pretty poor child he sleeps on thru this dreadful time, we should be thankful.*

Lieut Warnford, a relation of Rev Warnford Vicar of Dudwell did a fine feat, he attacked a Zeppelin and succeeded in dropping bombs onto it and destroyed it, the explosion, turned his monoplane upside down, but he succeeded in looping the loop and came down safely but in the enemy country. He quickly adjusted his machine and restarted and got safely back to headquarters. For this plucky feat the King has given him the V.C. A few days after this heroic feat he was killed trying a new flying machine.

13 June

Harvey and Gladys, Frank and his sister called. Will took Ma to Todmorden, he then took Uncle John Crossley onto Blackpool.

Good rest today, I took my Wordsworth and read a many of his beautiful poems. This horrid war gets on ones nerves and for a short time, how soothing it feels to get back, to read all that is beautiful in nature, no poet ever gave better expression in verse, peaceful times better than he.

14 June

Heavy fighting in the Dardanelles. This has been a costly affair both men and money, but will repay us in the end, but it seems a long way off yet.

15 June

Another Zeppelin raid today on the NE coast. Newcastle but the press is very reticent. Premier in the House today told us that we are spending 3 millions a day.

16 June

Halifax in the morning with Will to get my hair cut, nobody can cut it like Mr Day, these fellows here can only cut it short and leave a tuft on the forehead which is horrid. Todmorden casualties in the Dardanelles have been very heavy. Rain wanted very badly.

17 June

The Germans have suffered heavily at the hands of the Russians in spite of the rosy Berlin messages.

M J got a new watch Bracelet.

Before the war almost no wrist watches were worn, the fob watch being the preferred timepiece. The war required a convenient and reliable means for the troops to tell the time and the resulting popularity of the wrist watch extended to the general population and continued after the war.

18 June

The whole nation will mourn the grievous news today that Lieut Warnford V.C. the intrepid airman who singlehanded destroyed a Zeppelin last week has been killed in France while testing a new aeroplane. Anniversary of the Battle of Waterloo 100 years. Let us hope our troops will make another Waterloo today.

19 June

Mrs Eastwood to tea. Stayed at home too tired. How different time affects you when the hardest day was never too hard or the longest day too long.

20 June

M J and Will went to Todmorden after dinner.

22 June

Beautiful day, we all attended Miss Radcliffe (Gwendoline) Wedding to Dr Sharp at St John Church. It was a pretty wedding. The Church was packed, after the ceremony Luncheon was served in the school room and it was beautifully decorated. The place was filled with guests music during luncheon. After that we went up to Hazeldean and spent part of the evening. They were the recipients of a large number of beautiful presents, we met a lot of old friends and thoroughly enjoyed ourselves with all good wishes for their happiness.

23 June

Afraid I got cold yesterday the cutting wind up at Hazeldene was more than I could stand.

24 & 25 June

Not much progress just now, either way the French have done some good work this last few days.

<u>War Loan</u> The nation, now rich and poor will have a chance of helping in the War by subscribing to this fund. £5 is the

lowest bond and this can be paid in at so much per month. I think it will be compulsory, it ought to be. People that can patronize the Palace & Picture Houses 2 or 3 times per week can do this. This war will alter many things, it will take the swelled head out of the British workman in general.

26 June

The much needed rain fell today this will do incalculable good. Will took Ma to Halifax in the car. I suffered terrible today from toothache.

27 June

Will ran over to Oldham to see Harvey. M J went to Hipperholme to see the Misses Greenwood. J Noble & George Wood came on this evening, we had a good chat on the old nigger times.

28 June

Thunder today. We are deeply sorry to hear that Capt Graham (Annie Briggs) husband killed in action, poor girl words fail me. He was in a Northumberland Regiment. He was mentioned in dispatches by Sir John French.

Captain H G Graham was killed in action on 24th June 1915 while serving with the 5th Battalion Northumberland Fusiliers. He was married in October 1914 to Annie Briggs of Elland. He is buried in St Quentin Cabaret Military Cemetery, near Ypres, Belgium.

29 June

Thunderstorm, but the rain will do much good.

30 June

No particular news today. We get wearied waiting day by day. Time going rapidly, and progress going slow. Munitions now going on rapidly, every town of importance are doing something, we must have high explosive shells at all cost to end this horrid war.

CALIS
POISON
Matt's Capital Cartoon
MATT

1 July

Good progress made in the Dardanelles.

2 July

Leyland Liner sunk today off the Scilly Isles, by a German Submarine. Had 1½ offered for 2/24 laps today but could not accept until some of my Contracts run out.

3 July

Harvey & Frank came this afternoon. Harvey has joined the O.T.C. (Officer Training Corps). *He goes on Monday.*

4 July

Very heavy wet day. Will took Mr Richardson to preach to Coley in sidecar, he could not get there in time any other way. Harvey & Frank went home tonight.

5 July

Dull day. Papers predict the War will end by October. Germans are said to be making another supreme effort to get to Calais, they are massing troops for that purpose.

6 July

How we all clamour for our morning papers, and still not much progress made. It got on our nerves to think how in the end it will alter all our lives as it were politically, socially and in many other ways it brings to mind the Bible quotation we shall be all altered in the twinkle of an eye. I look with a grave face to our future for a long time. England has gone on in a go as you please fashion for a long time, liberty in my estimation is a dangerous thing to administer, and in the past few years we have been bountiful in this respect.

7 July

Many merchant ships have been torpedoed this week, this is becoming very serious to us.

Time and tide wait for no man but woman puts the clock back and rides over the tide.

8 July

Another birthday comes round today. How long can I keep it up at the rate we are going today?

9 July

Russia's smashing blow. Austro-German Armies in retreat. Capture of 11,000. The entire German forces in S.W. Africa have surrendered to Gen Botha & hostilities have now ceased, this will relieve part of our army to come to Europe.

I sent the usual P.C sketch to B Sutcliffe whose birthday is the day after mine. I am sorry to say he has not been well for some time back but I hope he will pull thro.

My last Birthday Sketch to B Sutcliffe.

10 July

Mrs Eastwood to tea Ran down to Brighouse called to see Mr & Mrs Manly saw many others.

Sorry to hear my other friends Benj Sutcliffe and Sam Briggs are very ill indeed.

11 July

Upset today, Tom Wood & Broadbent got to words & blows over some hens, it was a low blackguardly affair.

Will ran Mr Richardson up to Barkisland to preach the Anniversary Sermon.

Our old friend Sam Briggs I am sorry to record died this afternoon, he has been ailing for the last few months, I only saw a few days ago but saw in him a great change, but still he passed his usual joke, as he always did when you came into his company. I have known him a very very long time, when he lived at Greetland he married John Ely sister Elizabeth and I have been in touch with him more or less all my life. His Father did not leave him anything when he died, thru some difference they had which I always considered very unfair. He then came to Elland & started in the Confectionary business, which developed to public catering etc etc and are known far & wide. He had a most happy disposition and was a great favourite in the town for his genial companionship. We shall miss a dear old friend who has linked us on in a very happy past.

Sam Briggs died aged 76, he left a widow and five children. For his daughter, Annie, this was another blow as her husband Captain Graham had only recently been killed in action (see entry for 28 June).

12 July

"Warp Heads" Annual Outing to "Coxwold".

13 July

Rather tired today. Glad to get back to business, we are very busy, margins are going up, if we had only plenty of hands we could shift some stuff. Everything you use gone up in price.

14 July

Attended the funeral of my old friend Sam Briggs at Elland Cemetery it was a very quiet affair, service in the Parish Church by Canon Winter. German Bankers I see are beginning to feel the pinch, if the War holds on much longer the Germans will be bankrupt.

15 July

Showery all day. The Germans according to one writer in today's paper says the Germans have made more shells in one day than England has made in a year, this shows what a definite stand she can make.

16 July

<u>Welsh Colliery Strike</u> the men both defy their Leaders & the Government knowing the need of coal we require for our fleet, they dare do such a thing. This shows what Trade Unions are doing to the country.

17 July

Rather cool today. Went to Greetland Church afternoon with M J called coming home at Mrs Briggs.

Talking with a well known Monumental Sculptor, Mr Noble he was saying that he is called upon to put the most absurd Epitaph etc on monuments, it reminds me of one writer who says

Few men go into Heaven in the face value of their Epitaph – and fewer women

Beauty may only be skin deep, but no man wants it to be deeper.

Marriage like the poor, will ever be with us.

18 July

Will took Ma to Oldham after dinner. I stayed indoors, had a good rest. Evening we went to St Johns West Vale. Mr Richardson preached.

19 July

Benj Sutcliffe I was sorry to hear was seriously ill. War news very scarce today. Cold weather.

20 July

Warsaw in the balance. The German Austrian troops are making desperate efforts to get there but I hope the Russians will be too many for them.

21 July

Welsh Miners have been soothed down by a 10% advance, this cannot go on forever. They are the best paid workmen in the country and they are never satisfied. War news very scant. America looks at last like coming to a final decision. Germany as usual has evaded the real question again, so we wait events.

The Isle of Man is suffering very much practically the Hotels & Boarding Houses are almost at a standstill, only 1 Boat going a day & this going at great risk, it will ruin hundreds.

The decision mentioned above refers to America's reaction to the sinking of the RMS *Lusitania.*

22 July

Almost finished my Sketch for the "Warp Head" "Postcard". They take a lot of time to do and nothing for doing it only the love of the thing. Perhaps somebody appreciates them, one never knows. I gave the original sketch to Mr Bob Wood, he for one appreciates some for he has them all mounted & framed.

William often created postcards of his sketches to commemorate significant local events, sometimes for his own amusement and sometimes by commission. The postcards are now considered collector's items.

23 July

Halifax tonight to get hair cut. Called at West Vale coming home. Saw T Sutcliffe told me Benjamin was very ill indeed but thought he would pull thru.

24 July

Alexander Rose Day today for this district girls out early this morning succeeded in selling a rose to every person they saw & they were very active all day. The proceeds go to the Royal Infirmary.

25 July

Beautiful morning. Will took Ma to Malham today they started off 10.30.

26 July

Oppressive day and work was difficult we have got 1 Twiner on 2/20 cheeses & it keeps us going and proper. We could not do it in cops.

27 July

Close day. Russians making a stubborn stand before Warsaw, this is a very trying battle. If Germany can gain the day, it will give her liberty with troops for the West, but she will just miss her calculations.

British Casualties to date. Total of 321,889 Killed, Wounded & Missing. This painfully reminds us of the serious nature of the great task we are engaged upon, and are a long way off the finish.

28 July

Busy day. With all twiners on heavy count it fell very hard on Will & myself. We could do with a little help but at the price of wages just now it's impossible.

A man drift into marriage but a woman dives in.

You never know what you can't borrow until you try.

29 July

M J not so well, keeps having a most violent pain after partaking of her meals, it makes us very uneasy.

30 July

Oppressive day, thunder hanging about. Good prices again offered today but cannot accept until present Contracts are out.

31 July

Ernest Jagger neighbour of ours returned on leave from the front, we were all delighted to see him, for months he has been in the thickest of the fighting, he intends to be married before he goes back.

The hand that rules a man makes him rock the cradle.

The hand that rules a man makes him rock the Cradle

1 August

Afternoon to Savile Park to the Drum Head Service, just when the troops assembled there came a regular deluge so they had to dismiss them. Went to St Johns in the evening. Geo & Hilda were there & came on home with us.

2 August

Started the last twiner on Cheeses. Have now got them all changed, it's an expense and I hope it will pay for it.

3 August

Most oppressive weather, a stifling heat, I never rested one minute from 6.30 to 6.30 and doing downright manual labour & grumbled at that.

4 August

Close day. Evening Service St Johns West Vale. Intercession Services Anniversary of the Declaration of War. Mr Richardson preached an eloquent sermon and I was repaid for going.

Framed 4 of the "Warp Head" Postcards and hung it in the passage.

The Intercession Service was for the troops and the successful conclusion of the war.

5 August

Not so well today but I had to do the usual hard work and at close I was played out, this cannot last forever, it's all in the game. Fall of Warsaw. The Russians have evacuated the city in perfect order.

6 August

Thank God we finish tonight and for a week we can rest our weary bones, and are out of the din & rattle, and the daily bickerings of the workpeople, this last 12 months has been the hardest I have ever known.

7 August

Holidays start today. So did the rain, it simply poured all day and far into the night, so we all stayed at home and glad to do that in these trying times. Many people are off to the seaside for all that.

8 August

Showery all day & toward night it poured down. I pity all the folks who are away on their holidays if the weather is like this, it is miserable. We are caged up like wild beasts.

9 August

Showery. Showery all morning but towards afternoon it cleared. M J & Will went out for a spin. Mr F Smith from Rochdale called on business bent, he gave us a better price for further contract. National Registration Act were handed in to every householder in the United Kingdom, this is to get to know exactly what available men we have to fill the ranks if required.

The National Registration Act was a census of the adult population. By the spring of 1915 volunteers for the army were drying up so the Government decided to find out exactly what manpower was available.

10 August

Afternoon we all started for Todmorden on the sidecar, myself riding on the back. I endured the agony as far as Luddenden Foot then took the train, no more thank you. Heavy downpour during journey.

11 August

I stayed at Woodlands, the weather was fickle so dare not go out, but spent the time with a good book JW having plenty. Reading Charles Dickens "Hard Times".

12 August

Walk down Todmorden in the morning, it was very bright, saw nothing of note. Rain fell again afternoon, so got back to my book.

13 August

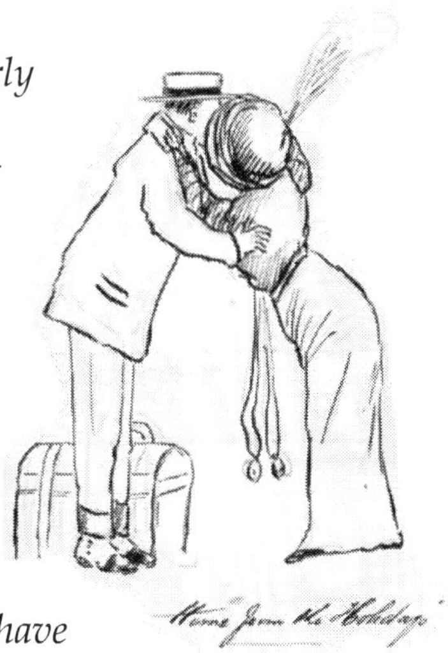

Beautiful morning, short walk, then early dinner and left for home, having had a very good rest & I feel much better. Got home & found Will struggling with the Motor Cycle, the bearings gone wrong so he will be held up a few days.

14 August

As usual thunder showers, thus ends our holidays. They have not been pleasant owing to the weather, but the rest will have done us good & make us fit for the very heavy work we have ahead of us, and winter with its trying weather will try all our strength.

15 August

Bright morning. Bertha came by the early morning train. Thunderstorm afternoon. M J & B went up to see Mrs Rothwell.

16 August

National Register Papers out today. This is to get a precise number of eligible men that can be called upon for service.

17 August

Depressing news today loss of a Transport in the Dardenelles. 1,000 lives, this is a sad blow but it's the first loss we have had in this department & we have moved millions of troops.

18 August

The 4 W.R. Regiment have had a severe engagement, and a many lads from our district have fallen. Capt. Andrews Head Master Hipperholme Grammar School & one from Elland. Two Wilson Liners torpedoed.

19 August

The White Star "Arabic" sunk today by submarine off the Irish Coast. 49 lives lost. 374 were rescued.

Capt. Andrews Head Master Hipperholme Grammar School was shot, while giving assistance to a wounded soldier. This inhuman method is sure to bring its own retribution.

Captain Maynard Percy Andrews, the headmaster of Hipperholme Grammar School, was killed in action on 15th August 1915. William's description of his death is substantially correct. He was, along with others, attempting to rescue a seriously wounded man. He is buried in Colne Valley Cemetery, Ypres, Belgium.
The 4th Battalion West Riding Regiment, the local territorial battalion, had arrived in France in April 1915. After their initiation into trench warfare in a quiet sector in France, they were sent to the Ypres Salient in July 1915 where they found conditions very different.

20 August

Bad news again today. Russia seems to have had a severe loss, if the reports to hand today are true. Received a letter from Mrs Eastwood, Hilda & George. They are off for their holiday in N. Wales.

21 August

Depressing news again today. Naval Engagement in the Baltic. Russians lost 3 Ships. Will went to spend the weekend with Harvey. This I think the blackest week since the war commenced. Selling Marguerites today for the Wounded Soldiers.

22 August

Restful day. Italy I am glad to say has decided to come in with the Allies & declared War on Turkey.

23 August

Better news today. German Naval Disaster, in the Riga fight, have lost 1 Dreadnought 2 Cruisers & 8 Torpedo boats. German losses up to date is estimated at 2,000,000.

24 August

Beautiful day. The moon was at full tonight and it was very beautiful. Heavy naval firing off the Belgian coast.

25 August

Reported in the Evening paper that we had got thru the Dardenelles. I hope this is correct.

The report was incorrect, there was no breakthrough and there would not be one as will be seen.

26 August

Beautiful day. M J went to Hipperholme to see Miss Greenwoods.

27 August

M Jane not so well today.

28 August

Harvey came this morning to spend the weekend, he has not got his Commission yet but daily going to the Manchester University to complete his studies. Will took him to Bolton Woods in the afternoon.

M J and myself went to Halifax to see "What the Butler Saw" A most laughable Comedy & for 2 hours it raised our depressed spirits somewhat, but for all that we felt out of place, but these times are miserable.

29 August

Stayed at home all day. New suit on today.

30 August

No news of any importance today from the front. M J & Will ran up to Todmorden tonight, found Bertha somewhat better but not right yet.

31 August

Russians retreating and as they do they destroy all communications, some towns they burn, they are playing the old Russian game they did with Napoleon. Let us hope the Kaiser will follow suit.

1 September

Benj Sutcliffe sorry to hear is in a very critical way, saw his Brother tonight.

Heavy fighting in the Dardanelles, this has been one of the toughest jobs we have had to tackle & we have lost heavily on troops but hopes are held out that we should be thru with it in a few weeks, but the suspense is terrible.

2 September

Very frosty early morning, does this predict a bad winter, I hope not we have anxiety enough without this.

3 September

Ran up Stainland tonight to see Mr Taylor on behalf of I E Ingham.

4 September

Beautiful morning. Will took his Mother to Blackpool they started off about 12 o'clock. I went to Huddersfield, had a look round then came home, saw a number of wounded soldiers.

5 September

I feel lost today, but I kept myself busy in getting all my accounts booked up and that took me almost all the day. With an interesting book I got thru the latter part very well.

6 September

M J & Will got back this afternoon detained on the road by punctures. They have enjoyed their short stay but the place is crowded. Allan Liner "Hesperion" torpedoed off the Irish Coast.

The RMS *Hesperion*, a passenger liner, was torpedoed on 4th September 1915 with the loss of 32 lives by the same U Boat which had sunk the RMS *Lusitania*. Ironically the body of Frances Stephens, one of the victims of the Lusitania, was being returned home giving her the dubious distinction of having been sunk twice by the same submarine captain.

7 September

Harrison Liner torpedoed today but crew saved. Busy day twiner off as per usual suffering from Lloyd George.

I have been busy of late bottling Fruit. I am very fond of fruit, and I think we should preserve as much as we can at this time of the year as will last us thru the winter months at a little cost, but just now sugar is a costly thing to what it was a year ago. However, I have bottled, Rhubarb (cherries my favourite) plums, greengages, damsons. I hope they will be successful. I had no failures last year.

Mode - Put your fruit into glass pressure jars, put these in the oven & heat the fruit up to nearly boiling point. Then take them out & pour boiling water into the bottles & fill well up over the fruit & then have a stiff starch paste ready & paste 6 or 7 layers of paper on the bottles while they are hot. These then will act like a board & will keep well in a cool place until the winter months. Of course there are bottles specially made with screw stoppers, I have these, but the other way will do equally well if you have not these.

T&J Harrison were a Liverpool based shipping company which ceased trading in 2002. They lost 27 ships during the war.
Lloyd George, the Liberal Chancellor of the Exchequer, had introduced sick pay for workers, a measure which William heartily disapproved of believing it to encourage absenteeism.

9 September

Visitors today. Flora & Bertha Maud & her two girls came to see us. Maud was looking very well, and the girls were two treats full of life, they enjoyed the short stay & went home by the 7 train.

Tom Whiteley, better known as "Scrabo" called to see me, not seen him for a very long time, the last time was on the Great Eastern when he was at Liverpool during the Exhibition, he has a show on Board.

Additional Note: Great Eastern designed by Isambard Kingdom Brunel in 1853, the largest ship of its day.

Tom Scrabo Was a West Vale lad & know him very well. I think he worked once for my Father, but left working & started hawking with a pack, but gave that up. He was a member of the West Vale Brass Band and played the Euphonium and this started him on the road. Along with another member of the band they went off busking. After a time they joined Old Rhodes Theatre and were the chief of the Orchestra. The next time he turned up was with a Fat Woman Show & he travelled all the Fairs etc. His next show was a Giant Horse & this lasted a few months, then he had other shows. He became partner in Allsops Great Waxwork Show in Liverpool with a branch in Manchester. He told me he lost £3000 with this, but started on the road again & got onto his pins again and he has made money so he tells me & has left his business with one of his sons. He at present is running 2 Cinema Shows in Manchester.

11 September

Left here 6.30 for Blackpool. Arrived late 10.15. Missed meeting JW & Mary but found them later. Stayed with them Star Cliffe Cornwall Avenue Mrs Flood. I went to the Tower Circus afternoon but nothing of any note. Vera Robinson acting as Conductor on the Blackpool Trams.

12 September

A most beautiful bright sunny day. We went for a walk to Norbreck, the cliffs were in as full as on a Bank Holiday. The town never as full at this date before, walk in the evening.

13 September

Went with John Walter by car to Fleetwood but could not get near the docks, all guarded. Saw a Steamer sailing for Douglas with some Germans aboard to be detained there in camp. We crossed the ferry to Knot End & pretty village, had luncheon at the Hotel there and they did us well. We had a most enjoyable day came home by train. I left at 7.5 for home arrived 11.30.

There were 2 internment camps on the Isle of Man where German civilians were imprisoned, one at Knockaloe on the west coast near Peel and a smaller one at Douglas.

We saw a Norwegian Ship brought into Fleetwood taken by patrol boat loaded with oil for German Submarines, this makes the second prize ship brought into Fleetwood.

The Norwegian ship was stopped as part of the British blockade of Germany. Neutral ships were stopped and searched for materials which would be useful to Germany and if any were found the ships were escorted to a British port and the goods confiscated. Not surprisingly this was not popular with neutral governments and care had to be taken not to antagonise them too much.

15 September

Very hot day, it was very trying in the mill.

16 September

Nothing new today from the front. Russians have taken a large number of prisoners again. We learn now how it was the Russians had to retreat, the Russian Munition Arsenal was blown up by

German Spies. Also a German Officer had been on the staff all along with the Grand Duke & revealed all his movement but he was shot.

17 September

Very hot oppressive day. Many transatlantic ships of late when getting into mid ocean has taken fire. German devilry at work again.

18 September

Fine afternoon. Will took Ma for a short spin. Went to West Vale last night bought some whisky on the strength that next week it will be higher.

There used to be a milestone at the Royal Oak at Halifax, it was taken up by the Corporation for the purpose of renewing the inscription.

To London 198 Miles

Huddersfield 7

Sheffield 31

The only other stone in the district which tells the distance to London is the one at Blackshaw Head at the junction of the Colden road with the main road.

Uncle John Crossley very busy just now with his Greenhouse, getting a regular florist.

19 September

Reading "He went out with the tide" by Guy Eden a good book but a sorrowful ending. Will took Ma to Todmorden brought our Bertha back.

20 September

Will not so well today, should have gone to Rochdale but not fit. Frank Smith came. Flora came back with Will.

21 September

John Hartley of Clock Almanack fame was married today, this will be his 3rd wife, he is 76. I think something else has taken possession of his brain besides poetry.

John Hartley (1839-1915) was a Halifax born poet who wrote in the Yorkshire dialect. His third wife, Annie Spencer, a former Hebden Bridge school mistress travelled all the way from Canada to marry him so he obviously had something going for him.

22 September

Reported from one MP that 40 German Submarines have been sunk.

23 September

Budget Day. A sensational Budget but of course this high debt will have to be met.

Tea from	*8d to 1/- per lb*
Coffee	*2 to 3*
Chicory	*1 to 1½*
Cocoa	*1 to 1½*
Sugar	*½ per lb*
Currants	*2 to 3/- per cwt*
Tobacco from	*4/8 to7/-*

½ Stamps abolished

Income Tax

Petrol

Tax on over 55/- per week

In all 106 Millions in Extra Taxes

Russians have recovered their retreat and are holding up the Germans again. Bulgaria are mobilizing their army but on which side they will fight is not clear yet, they say armed neutrality. M J very ill all day, she was upset last night by the brute next door Broadbent, he was thrashing unmercifully his little child 15 months old. His wife pleading for it & screaming for her life. M J ran down the street to fetch his Aunt to quell this monster. They have got another baby 3 weeks ago. He was shaking that the other day. M J gave him a dressing down told him if it occurred again she would inform the officer for the Suppression of Cruelty to Children.

25 September

Fine clear day but rather colder. Will took M J for a short run in the afternoon. I went to Halifax to Matinee "Potash & Perlmutter". I enjoyed it very much, really a two horse piece, they were both very good indeed.

Additional note: Advert for "Potash & Perlmutter" at Theatre Royal week 20th September, Halifax Courier. An Enormously Successful Character Comedy in Three Acts. The play that is making all London laugh.

26 September

Todmorden with Will in the afternoon at Mytholmroyd we met the West Riding Regiment they had been on a 300 mile recruiting march. West Vale in the evening St Johns Harvest Festival. Mr Eastwood, Hilda & George there, also Mr Arthur Law. The font was beautiful, a wealth of flowers by Mildred Law.

27 September

Allies great move in the west. Germans driven back all along western line. 14,000 prisoners captured & many guns. French fighting like demons. Germans repulsed at Dvinsk. Ivanoff's success in the south. 10,600 more prisoners. So today we are proud of our great victories, but let us not be too jubilant.

28 September

Further news came also today of the Great Victory by the British & French in the west, the effect of the French Artillery was terrific & completely paralysed them, the Germans cried for mercy. The fighting at close quarters was terrible, and the ground was one mass of mutilated bodies. It is thought the French used some gaseous shells, so they are getting some of their own devilled work back again. The troops are all in excellent spirits at their success. Berlin Wireless as usual puts the victory the other way round, they are afraid of Germany getting to know the exact truth.

The battle of Loos had started on 25th September and after an encouraging start it descended into the usual stalemate before ending in the middle of October with very little gain. It featured the first use by the British of poison gas. There was criticism of the British Commander in Chief, Sir John French, for not allowing the reserves to move up in sufficient time and he was eventually replaced by Douglas Haig.

29 September

Mrs A W Law took the beautiful Floral Cross from the Font at the Harvest Festival up to Greetland Church & placed it on our beloved Arnold's grave, this kind remembrance & sympathy touches us deeply. Mrs Law took one last year.

30 September

The push forward in France is making good progress. Further gains being reported today. Sir John French says our men captured in all 3,000 prisoners & 40 guns. The French took 900 prisoners. Loos – Latest report of the great Battle in the West. The German losses in killed, wounded & prisoners exceed the strength of 3 Army Corps about 120,000 men.

1 October

Bulgaria looks like threatening to us if she sides with Germany which at the moment looks like, it will mean a heavy burden on us. It will be a heavy blow again as in our fight for the Dardanelles.

2 October

Rather dull today. Will ran me up to Outlane to see the recent excavations at "Cambodunum", the site of a Roman Camp. For a long time this has gone on, the additional excavations of the boundary walls are very interesting.

3 October

Arnold's Day I went to West Vale Church morning, stayed for Communion. Mr Diggle preached instead of Dr Jowett. I liked his sermon very much. Will ran him home after service. M J & Will went to Evening Service.

4 October

Busy day as usual another hand chucked work so shall have to do the best we can until we get another.

5 October

Germans making desperate efforts to get back their lost ground but are foiled every attempt with heavy losses. Bulgaria at last going to help Germany this will add somewhat to our difficult task in the Dardanelles.

6 October

Greece against her own people is going to remain neutral, but I cannot see how this can be managed, she is really bound in honour if Serbia is attacked to help her. I wonder if this is another Scrap of paper. Will received a long letter from Frank at the front. Up to now he is alright but it's awful work he says but he says he feels safe.

7 October

West Vale tonight for an hour or two called at the Shears, as usual some of the boys there.

Knowledge is power; and yet on old maid is single because she knows too much.

8 October

Another pay day over, these are days we have got a dread of because always somebody going to leave or asking more wages. One man I am paying 30/- per week for a 18/- a week job, had the cheek to ask for 32/- and I am afraid I shall have to give it him, as there are no hands to do job.

9 October

Dull day. M J went to Hipperholme.

10 October

Dull day. Went to spend the evening with Mr & Mrs Cockcroft neighbours of ours who have gone to live at a "Bungalow" at top of Ainleys. I was much taken with it and wish I could afford to build one on the same lines.

11 October

Butter 1/9 per lb so we are going to change to Margarine, we cannot afford Butter.

12 October

Went to Halifax to get my hair cut. Called at West Vale coming home.

13 October

Another Zeppelin raid on London 40 killed.

In the House of Commons today it was mooted that half our incomes will be taken for war purposes, this looks black but before the War is over more drastic things than this will have to be done, the workman will have to realize his position, as he did in the past. He is only a workman but legislation for the past 10 or 15 years have put him on a pedestal and now he has got position of the situation, and just now they will only do what they think is enough, & insult you in at the bargain. Cart drivers in Elland with 1 horse start today at 30/- per week & start at 7 o'clock in the morning. If prices like these for unskilled men, what about skilled labour, revolution will come, sooner & better I could see every devil starve, without pity.

Bulgarian & German reverses. Serbia putting up a great fight.

Bulgaria entered the war on 14th October following promises of territory from the Central Powers and attacked Serbia, her traditional enemy. This was the death knell for Serbia. Her army and much of the civilian population retreated to the Adriatic coast suffering many losses and were evacuated to the Greek Islands.

14 October

English Submarine doing good work in the Baltic.

15 October

Got over another pay day & thank God have had no grumbling this week.

16 October

John Walker & Mary came to spend the weekend with us. We went to Halifax in the evening to the Royal to see a new play "Peg O' My Heart" and it was a charming play, & well mounted.

17 October

We stayed at home all day. Will took Ma & Aunty Mary to Greetland. JW stayed with me.

18 October

John Walter went home early morning but he had to come back to Halifax on business, so came here again. He brought Will a lovely edition, Scotts "Talisman", he had overlooked his birthday.

19 October

Dull day, frosty. Received letter from John Walter, he sent me the words of the song I have long wanted, "Katey Moyle" a song that our Jimmy use to sing.

20 October

Bad news tonight our Regiment the Duke of Wellingtons have suffered heavily in the last engagement. We are afraid to open the paper for fear of someone who we know has gone under. This daily tension is terrible.
<u>The King</u> today makes an appeal in all the papers for recruits, he says, the end is not yet in sight.
Great indignation all over the World over the Murder of Miss Cavell. A National Service at St Pauls attended by Queen Alexandra & Queen Mary & all distinguished Men & Women of London.

Edith Cavell, a British nurse working in Belgium, was executed by the Germans on 12th October 1915 for helping British, French and Belgian soldiers to escape. Although she was undoubtedly guilty of the crime the punishment was condemned around the world. Once again the Germans had scored a propaganda own goal.

On 16th October the 1/4th Battalion West Riding Regiment, the local territorial battalion, were involved in their first real fight since arriving in the Ypres sector. After a 3 hour bombardment the Germans launched a raid on an exposed part of the British trenches which was successfully repulsed. Casualties were 14 killed and 24 wounded which at the time seemed heavy.

21 October

Heard today the death of Charlie Stocks, West Vale. He worked for us at Victoria Mills and after the fire, he went with me to Brighouse many years. He was a good fellow & he was always reliable. I had always the highest respect for Charlie and we were always good friends. He did one many kindnesses that I cannot forget. He has suffered for a long time from Rheumatics. He died at Buxton where he had gone for treatment.

"Trafalgar Day"

22 October

Benjamin Sutcliffe died today after a long illness, another link broken in a lifelong friendship. We both went to the same school in early life and that friendship has never been broken. He was a man of sterling worth, his good sound judgement made him many friends and his loss touches me deeply. He was a man for whom I had the greatest esteem, his birthday was the day after mine & we always exchanged the best of wishes. I generally sent him some little thumb nail sketch. He left £7,539 gross with £6,425 net.

23 October

The loss of two friends this week, made me very despondent today & quite upset me. Went to Halifax with M J but nothing seemed to please me, so came home.

24 October

Went to the Lecture. Our folks ran to Todmorden this afternoon. Harvey & Harry Street came in their car just after they had left. They stayed a while then followed them.

I went to Halifax to hear Mr Wells lecture on the "Vatican". It was a capital lecture on one of the most wonderful buildings in the

World. The views were beautiful and its history was told with a masterly style. Its influence just now with its 183 Millions will have some effect on this horrible war.

25 October

Cold showery day. I paid my last respects to my old friend Benjamin Sutcliffe. Service was held in St John Church. Dr Jowett & the Vicar took the service. Mrs Turner played Dead March & on leaving the Church, O Rest in the Lord. A large number of friends were present.

26 October

Mr Eastwood & Hilda came on tonight.

27 October

West Vale St Johns tonight. At Home with M J glad to see a few old friends there but they are getting less. We stayed until 10 o'clock. The King who has gone out to visit our troops in France was thrown from his horse, the horse reared & fell back. The King was badly bruised.

28 October

M J went to St Johns again tonight but did not stay long. Recruiting just now I am pleased is going strong, it looks very much like Conscription in some form or other but I hope for the best. If Will has to go my trade will be ruined. I cannot at my time of life cope with the work.

29 October

Heavy dull day.

30 October

Dull cold miserable day. This has been one of our black weeks of the War. The junction effected between Germany & Bulgaria, the "impasse" in Gallipoli, resignation of French Cabinet, our own dissensions & the loss of the Argyll in this dark hour. Before the dawn?

The shortage of manpower at home caused by the enlistment of men into the army gave unprecedented employment opportunities for women. This acceptance of a greater role for women in society during the war undoubtedly helped their demands for suffrage.

31 October

Dull day. M J went to Mrs Eastwoods. Joe Noble came on in the evening.

1 November

Severe fighting again in the West. The Germans have retaken some trenches we took last week, at a fearful cost. The Balkan situation is now looking very serious.

2 November

Mr Asquith made a capital speech in the House, he trounced his critics and gave the country some of our difficulties that we could not foresee.

3 November

Nothing very important from the Front tho fighting for trenches taken & retaken occur daily. Will very ill today. He seems quite run down, we are much concerned for him.

4 November

Great indignation at the attitude of Greece who by Treaty should in honour go to the aid of the Serbians are remaining neutral, of course the Queen of Greece is the Kaisers daughter. Will not much better yet. He feels his position very much, we cannot spare him from the business to join the colours and he is afraid to go out & be called a Shirker, he would gladly go & fight for his country but in leaving us he would lose all.

5 November

M J had a very bad attack & for a time we were much afraid, sort of cramp in the stomach, this has troubled her for some time now.

6 November

Dull cold day. M J & Will ran up to Greetland with flowers, then home for the rest of the day. 900 Young Irishmen were sailing from Liverpool today to evade conscription. The crew refused to work the ship so they had to go back home.

A large number of Wounded Soldiers have come to St Lukes Hospital this week. In fact, the place will soon be full. All other patients have been removed to the Workhouse Hospital. This is a sad sight to see, but it makes one shudder to think how many poor wounded men we shall see in the World for the next 50 years to come.

7 November

Halifax Lecture tonight Mr F Martin Duncan "The Lore of the Bee". Interesting and fascinating lecture, moving pictures of bees, working etc., what a wonderful study these interesting creatures are, some things he told us seemed almost incredible.

8 November

Cold Day. Lord Kitchener left for the Eastern part of Europe, with our all, trust goes with him. The situation there requires some tact. Greece will sit on the fence until she sees which way Germany goes. If she goes under then she will help the Allies not unless.

Although she had a treaty to assist Serbia if she was attacked by Bulgaria, Greece remained stubbornly neutral until June 1917 in spite of all the Allies efforts. This didn't stop the British & French from landing troops at Salonika in October 1915 and using Greece as a base to fight Bulgaria & Austria.

10 November

Bitter cold day. German submarines have got into the Mediterranean & have sunk many ships both British, Italian & French.

11 November

Conscription again looks like been forced on the country. Some modification will have to be exercised or the trade of the country will come to a standstill.

12 November

Bitter cold wet day. Snow fell 2 or 3 inches on the hills round here.

13 November

Cold again today. Will took Ma to Todmorden in the sidecar then forward to Oldham to spend the weekend with Harvey. I stayed at home.

14 November

Went to Todmorden by the noon train. Tea at John Walters. Will brought Harvey back with him. All the hills round Todmorden were covered with snow.

15 November

First snow this morning, the ground was very soon covered with a white mantle but towards noon it ceased. Working until 8 o'clock this week.

16 November

Slippery today and very winter like. No fresh War News today from our headquarters. Russia is doing very well.

17 November

Much anxiety prevails just now about Greece. The joint powers have now given her the straight lips if she betrays us again. Arnold's Birthday. Could not take up any flowers on account of the weather.

My favourite Tobacco "Coolie Cut Plug" has risen from 3d per oz to 5d. My curses on the Kaiser.

18 November

Amidst all the work & worry I find time to direct my thought somewhat & snatch a few hours reading "Dumas" Le Chevalier de Maison-Rouge, for real romance give one Dumas.

19 November

No particular news today. Serbians are putting up a good fight and are waiting for the Allies for help, which I hope will be soon, if not all the worse for Serbia. Greece just now is the main factor.

20 November

Cold day. Halifax evening to the Royal to see "Oh I Say" a farcical French comedy. It was very comical but I prefer something more sterling than this. No doubt at one time I should have been vastly pleased, we have others in our thoughts.

21 November

Cold cloudless day. We all stayed indoors reading. M J not so well in the evening.

22 November

Working until 8'oclock until Wednesday. Huddersfield Cars are now running with female collectors on account of so many men joining the colours. Further restrictions in Public Houses not open now until 12.30 to 2 pm then 6 to 9.30. You cannot buy whisky out of a public house under a Quart. Anybody ill you cannot get a drop of Brandy without a Drs Certificate. This I say is very unfair. The trade and all its dependants are heavily hit & spells ruin to thousands. The temperance wedge is been driven too tight.

The Licensing Regulations, first introduced earlier in the war to reduce the alleged drunkenness of munitions workers and soldiers, were now being tightened. Temperance was an important issue of the time with much of society's ills being blamed on drink, and a very vocal and influential temperance lobby were attempting to stop or restrict the sale of alcohol.

23 November

No particulars from the Western Front. They seem to be playing a waiting game, but between the lines I feel sure we are nearing the end. Germany begins to feel the pinch with been cut off and in the end it will be her ruin.

24 November

Harvey came today, he had come to Huddersfield to be measured for his Officers Uniform, so he stayed all night with us.

Bitter frost early morning, bed this sort of weather is very boring.

25 November

Greece between the Devil & the deep sea does not know what to do, but our Government have told him in simple language that he will have to toe the line.

26 November

Russia mobilising a huge army & they have now a plentiful supply of ammunition & are ready to attack the Bulgarians, so we are pushing all speed now to give the Turk his final coup. Italy is doing good work along with us.

27 November

Cold day frosty wind. Too cold to go anywhere so with "Barnaby Rudge" I stayed where it was warm & comfortable.

Greece still wobbling.

28 November

Cold frosty day. M J went to Mrs Rothwells. I stayed at home.

29 November

Cold wintery morning. Towards night we had rain & sleet. Very heavy day at the Mill. Heavy delivery of weft, we are getting all the weft possible, there will soon be a shortage owing to scarcity of hands etc. etc.

30 November

No war news of any note today.

1 December

Thaw today & much warmer. A resolution was moved & seconded at the Elland Council that C P Trevelyan MP be taken out and shot, for his pro German speeches, pity it could not be carried out.

C P Trevelyan was the Liberal MP for Elland. He had resigned from the Government in August 1914 in protest against the war and remained a vigorous opponent throughout the conflict.

2 December

Milder today.

4 December

Heavy wet day. Halifax tonight. M J was anxious to see The Royal Divorce. We had a good night. A Great Grandson of Napoleon took the part of his great ancestor. I had seen the play many times but just now it has special interest.

5 December

Dull wet day. Never left the house. It was the day of rest and I honoured it.

6 December

Regular soaker today it never ceased. We are much perplexed as what to do under "Lord Derby Scheme" whether to attest or not, we are between the devil & the deep sea, personally I think it a catch.

7 December

Rain as usual. No fresh war news.

8 December

In the East things are looking black. Our retirement before Bagdad is not rosy & Greece still hangs in the balance.

9 December

Very heavy fall of snow today but towards evening rain fell which made the roads & streets very bad, trams had a difficulty in keeping on the track. M J went to Lightcliffe to see Major Sowerby, in a regular blizzard.

10 December

Exceptional heavy day, rain fell in torrents and the streets were impassable. Lieut Frank Buckley came this afternoon he is over from France on 7 days leave. We could not get him to say a word about our position out there. I was much disappointed with him. By his looks he seems to have had a soft job.

11 December

Miserable cold wet day. I went to the Annual Exhibition (Arts & Crafts) Halifax, the pictures were less in numbers but better in quality. I was much pleased with it, some very good work.

Our suspense for the last few days has been very great. Lord Derby's Scheme closed on and all persons of military age are pressed to be attested before then, or else they cannot appeal to the Local Tribunal. It is a difficult problem, and has troubled us deeply, as it would be ruinous to our business if Will had to go to the front. He was obliged to attest, that of course makes him a soldier, so today I was terribly distressed when he had to go to Halifax, but he went & was passed by the Dr who found him fit.

The Derby, or Group Scheme, was a last ditch attempt to ward off conscription. Men were invited to attest, or sign up, after which they would be called up according to their Group, which was based on age and marital status. With Britain's non-militarist attitude many men believed that they should be exempt from military service for business or family reasons. There was a different attitude on the continent where conscription, even in time of peace, was commonplace and men expected to be called up in time of war no matter what the personal cost.

12 December

The lookout this morning very wintery snow fallen during the night. A very depressing day, we are all anxious now that Will has attested and our only hope is that his appeal may be successful.

13 December

Thaw set in today, roads are shocking. Greece has at last given way to allow our troops to pass thru their territory.

14 December

We are experiencing great difficulties now with the Railway Co. They are so shorthanded that they cannot cope with the traffic & stations are closed for days. Cannot take or receive goods.

15 December

Rather better day as regards weather. We are terribly hard worked just now, have the warehouse packed up to the top and all to lift & handle, its slavery we cannot go on like this for ever. We all want this horrid war ending. Railway Co are completely blocked owing to shortage of men, that they cannot cope with the traffic at all. Stations closed for goods days at once.

Irving Holt invalided home called to see us. He has been out at the front for about 10 months, he was a boy pal of our Will. He was wounded by the bursting of a shell in the cheek. He told us a pitiful story. He was one of about 400 out of his lot that went out, so we can judge of what he had gone thru. He said I have seen Hell, Ypres, he said is pitiful to see beautiful houses just left after been shelled, with all the furniture in etc., would make you cry. Trench work is fearful day after day, knee deep in water, with death staring you in the face every moment. He told of one day which he experienced when he almost wished he was shot, it was so horrible. But he said & I could not but admire the lad, I would not have missed it for a fortune, that, the true spirit of a brave boy. We were all delighted to see him, he looks no worse for his beauty mark which he should be proud of.

16 December

Very heavy fog all day. Nothing particular from the seat of War. Sir John French resigns the Command of the troops in the West to Sir Douglas Haig.

Following the unsuccessful Loos offensive, and some ill considered leaks to the press, Sir John French was replaced as Commander in Chief of the British Expeditionary Force. He became Commander in Chief Home Forces for the remainder of the war.

His successor, Sir Douglas Haig, has been reviled as a butcher and bungler although many historians now believe this to be untrue and that he was a competent commander who did the best that could be done under very difficult circumstances.

17 December

Dreadful fog today. Gas burning all day at the Mill & we had a very heavy day with deliveries of skeps etc., we are packed from floor to ceiling, the work is dreadful heavy & ceaseless.

18 December

John Hartley the well known poet & dialect writer died today at Liscard aged 76. He will always be identified with the Clock Almanac. Had a delightful musical afternoon, the Royal to hear O'Mara Opera Co in "Trovatore". The whole tone of the Co was very good, a capital augmented orchestra & they did credit to this one of the Gems of the Operas.

19 December

Dull day. Will took his mother to Todmorden afternoon.

21 December

We have been busy writing out our Appeal (Lord Derby's Scheme) to go before the Committee. We are very anxious that he may be exempted, but the matter is a very serious & momentous question of us.

22 December

Dull heavy thick fog with drizzly rain all day.

23 December

We were shocked tonight on opening the paper, the sudden death of Mrs Jowett, Coley Vicarage. She was a good worker on anything appertaining to Church & Schools, and was a great helpmate to her husband. Mr & Mrs Jowett did their greatest & best work in starting St Johns West Vale. The work was hard & long but they will always be remembered by this noble work. When they left it Church, School, Vicarage was all clear & part of an Endowment Scheme. This requires no further eulogy. Mrs Eastwood & Hilda came in the evening.

25 December

Heard no Carol Singers last night. Not a bit like Xmas. Stayed at home. Our Xmas Dinner was devoid of the festive dishes, but we're thankful for that, only wished some of our Tommies could have had it. Will took his Ma a short ride. The evening turned out wet so stayed in.

For the second consecutive year Christmas finds nearly all the World at war. Mothers mourn for gallant sons slain, yet rejoice in the part which they acted in the Drama of blood & iron.

Louis Raemackers the celebrated Cartoonist has a remarkable one just out. Doctor & nurse are retiring from a room in a humble cottage. On the bed lies the corpse of the wife and mother. The husband sits in his chair, overcome with sorrow while between his knees stands a sweet little child who says:- But Mother had done nothing wrong had she daddy?

<u>The Kaiser did this</u>. Until the crown is torn from this criminals head, until the earth shall be delivered from the curse of his ambition, the bells of Yule must be muffled and the joys of Xmas be postponed.

Louis Raemaekers (1869-1956) was a Dutch cartoonist famous for his anti German stance. After the Germans offered a reward for his body, dead or alive, he was forced to flee to England in 1916.

Maud sent her usual present. Will got a capital book, "Kitcheners Stories", she sent me & M J a capital postcard photo of Jack in khaki, he has joined the Lancashire Cadets OTC (Officer Training Corps)

26 December

Attended the Memorial Service at St Johns in Memory of Mrs Jowett.

27 December

Coley today with M J to the funeral of Mrs Jowett. It was a very large funeral, the whole parish looked to be there. A good number of the West Vale St Johns were also present. The floral tributes were innumerable. Dr Baume, Archdeacon Norris & many other clergymen were present. Dr Jowett, I was sorry to see this following a few weeks sickness, has left him very ill indeed. The day was threatening but it kept fine until after the ceremony then it came down in torrents, with heavy wind we had difficulty in getting home. M J was taken badly coming home. This ends one of the saddest Xmas's I ever remember.

We attended this service to the memory of our dear friend Mrs Jowett. The Vicar Mr Richardson, who preached a beautiful sermon on St Stephen spoke of her great work in this beautiful Church. The great self sacrifice, in all her work in connection with the Parish, the sermon was very impressive.

The choir rendered the Hymns

432 My God my Father while I stray &

550 When the day of toil is done

with the greatest reverence & at the close Mrs Turner played the Dead March.

29 December

Harvey Street came yesterday, he looks very well indeed. Another shock this morning, our rent at the mill gone up another £20 per annum. Soaking day.

Ford the American Millionaire Peace Party has had to return to the States they are not wanted here.

Henry Ford of motor car fame was a committed pacifist and chartered a ship to send peace activists to Stockholm to sponsor a peace conference. None of the warring nations would attend so the attempt was unsuccessful. Henry Ford himself was forced to return to the USA due to illness.

30 December

New Year Greetings not as numerous as of yore. We only received one from Mr & Mrs Maitchell, Dewsbury. Received notice this morning from my landlord at the Mill for a further rise of £20 per year. This I shall be compelled to pay, but of the future this spells ruin to us, when normal prices come in.

31 December

Wild treacherous day. Thus ends the year, and one that will be handed down to posterity as one of the most awful of bloodshed, destruction, and sorrow, that the world has ever seen. Almost all Europe is in the grip of War and of its horrors & misery it will entail will take centuries to blot out. So let our prayers be for the coming Year the crowning triumph of our arms against the World & the Kaiser.

1916

The year 1916 would prove to be a watershed year for Great Britain. Her new volunteer citizen army would join the fray with mixed results and she would find it necessary to further erode the civil liberties that she was fighting so hard to protect.

The three great Allied Powers, Great Britain, France and Russia, had agreed late in 1915 that they would mount simultaneous offensives in the summer of the next year to stretch German resources to the limit and prevent them moving reserves from west to east and vice versa. The British proposal was for their new army to launch an attack in the Ypres area but the French were having none of that. They were deeply suspicious that the British would not pull their weight unless they could keep a close eye on them, so they insisted that the British attack alongside them where the French and British armies met astride the River Somme. The British commander-in-chief, Sir Douglas Haig, whose instructions from the government were to co-operate with the French, reluctantly agreed to their wishes and the scene was set for the infamous Battle of the Somme.

The Germans of course had ideas of their own. Their new commander Erich von Falkenhayn decided to target the French army and bleed them dry in a battle of attrition. He needed to find an objective that the French were not prepared to give up and where he could bring his superiority in artillery to bear. He chose Verdun and in February pre-empted the allied offensive by attacking in force. At first things went to plan but the French mounted a ferocious resistance and the German commanders on the spot committed more and more troops, contrary to Falkenhayn's plan, and their losses rose to the same levels as the French. The battle became a meat grinder for both sides and as French losses mounted it became clear that the Somme offensive was desperately needed to relieve the pressure. The French contribution was scaled back and the effort became a predominantly British one.

On the 1st July 1916, after a week of bombardment on the enemy entrenchments, Kitchener's men scrambled out of their trenches and advanced on the German positions. On the northern two thirds of the front it was an almost complete disaster with hardly any gains made. On the southern one third almost all of the objectives were gained with modest casualties. At the end of the day the army had suffered 20,000 dead with a further 40,000 wounded, the worst day in the history of the British army, with Kitchener's volunteers taking the brunt of the losses. With the ongoing struggle at Verdun and the simple fact that they were not going to defeat the German army by sitting in their trenches, the battle had to continue and so it did until November when the weather prevented any further activity. The initial stages had highlighted the deficiencies in training and lack of experience of the new army and also found that the newly expanded munitions industry at home had issues with quality control with many of the shells the artillery fired failing to explode. For all its inconclusive results, the battle did relieve the pressure on the French and proved a valuable, if costly, learning experience for the British army and also proved to be a trying experience for the Germans who suffered every bit as badly as the British and French.

The Russians lived up to their part of the bargain by attacking on the Eastern Front in June, the so called Brusilov offensive, which completely broke through the Austro-Hungarian lines advancing many miles and inflicting considerable casualties before it petered out in September and the front stabilised. Although the attack was a brilliant success it still did not gain a decisive victory and, by the end, much of the Russian army's offensive power was used up which did not bode well for the future.

At home 1916 saw one of the most controversial decisions of the war when conscription was introduced in January, at that time for single men only, later to be extended to all men of military age. The move was fiercely contested both in and out of Parliament but was eventually passed, although the Government had to include appeals on the grounds of conscience and so were born the conscientious objectors who have so fired the imagination of the British public. Of the appeals made against conscription only a very tiny percentage were on the grounds of conscience.

This year also brought about a change in government. Prime Minister Herbert Asquith had already been forced to form a coalition government in May 1915 and growing dissatisfaction with the conduct of the war and the seemingly unbreakable stalemate on the Western Front caused growing pressure on him to step down. Ever the political opportunist, Lloyd George intrigued ceaselessly to undermine Asquith's position and, after an orchestrated press campaign, Asquith resigned in December 1916 allowing him to take up the reins of power.

Thus begins one of the most eventful years in our history we know not what trials are in store for us, or what sorrow A new year is a dawn of hope we are struggling for justice, humanity and all that can be expressed by the sacred word Freedom, and may the year by the grace of God witness the dawn of Britain's greatest glory.

1 January

Dreadful gale with heavy rain today Loss of P&O steamer "Persia".

2 January

M J went to Todmorden by the 9:30 train I went to West Vale St Johns to Intercession service, District Councillors were present, also other bodies Mr Richardson preached an eloquent sermon, the service concluded by singing the National Anthem.

Thy ways are wonderful O God

Who makes wars to cease

Oh let this be the final war

That ushers in thy peace

Bishop Boyd Carpenter

3 January

German Submarines in the Mediterranean have sunk 3 Steamers.

4 January

Weather still boisterous. Nothing new from the front, our progress is very slow but very sure we are playing them a waiting game but it's a costly one.

5 January

Parliament today are called to consider compulsion, on the strength of a large number single men not attesting under Lord Derby Scheme. I hope this will not come into force it would degrade England.

Tell me what you like and I'll tell you what you are

The undertaker is very slow but very sure

Wild wet day.

Carl Rosa's Opera Co in this week. Sorry I have been unable to go see them.

6 January

<u>Conscription shelved</u>

The unattested have now to be called up to be attested like the first batch. Split in the labour ranks, this is the wrong time to change horses.

7 January

Russia now seems to be making headway, they have got ammunition & are massing a huge army & will soon strike a deadly blow in the East. The death of David Tong removes one of Elland's best known men, he was formerly Newsagent at the Cross and at one time had all the newspaper trade in the district. He was Secretary for Elland Cricket Club about 25 years. He was a member of the volunteers & was a crack shot. He was a musician of no mean order & a member of the Halifax Choral Society he played the Cello, for a long time I took lessons from him, when we started the West Vale Orchestra, I used to enjoy my lessons, he was a capital story teller, & well read man, I only had a chat with him a few week ago, and he said he was first rate in health but his legs were done, no wonder I said when you come to consider the mileage you have done in your daily business.

No man can be really appreciated but by his equals or superior

Ruskin (Modern Painter)

8 January

Better day, fine for a change, but we were all too tired to go out, so stayed in.

9-15 January

Missing from copy of diary.

16 January

Will ran up to Todmorden with his Mother. Bertha came here by the noon train. Mrs Eastwood, Hilda & George came on after service.

17 January

Will put back to the (12 Group), this only put off our anxiety a little longer, it is getting more than we can bear.

This is a reference to the Group or Derby Scheme of enlistment. Will had attested under this scheme and had now been placed in the 12th group of men who would be called up.

18 January

Surrender of Montenegro is a sad blow to the Allies, some writers infer we have been sold, time will prove this. Wills Birthday. Ma bought him a signet ring .

19 January

Heavy storm of rain & hail this evening. Dorothy playing at Halifax this week.

20 January

Still rough weather. Nothing new from the front the West still quiet, the East seems to be busy the Russians make steady progress, the position at Salonika is getting strengthened which will take a tremendous power to break.

21 January

Letter from Harvey, Clipstone Park.

22 January

John Walter, Mary came to spend the week end with us, the weather was cold so we did not go out at all. We played cards.

23 January

Brighter day, we had a very pleasant day, Will took J W a short run, but it was rather cold.

26 January

Halifax tonight to Literary Society.

Alex Keighley FRPS (Steeton) gave his Lecture " In an old Garden" he is well known in the Photographic World for his Art

Photography. I have seen many of his works from time to time at the Exhibitions. The slide show was of the highest order in fact I never saw better, commencing with the flowers of spring. He went all thru the seasons and under all conditions, each morning & evening, some charming snow & fog pictures were shown, I was delighted.

Noble act is nothing less than the expression of a great soul, & great souls are not common things
Ruskin

No great intellectual thing was ever done by great effort, a great thing can only be done by a great man, and he does it without effort
Ruskin

Our hopes are again down, this morning tells us that the 12th Group will be rolled up on the 3rd Feb, so we shall have to make another appeal.

27 January

Mr & Mrs Geary came in the evening he brought me a book, he is very fond of a good book & we exchange them, "Captains All" Jacob. Joe Noble came in evening as usual he was brimful of humour etc etc, he wore the (Derby Armlet) ie in place of the Crown it has a Bass's Ale Label, we had no end of fun.

William and his son were reluctant to allow him to be called up and were preparing an appeal for him to be exempted from service in the Armed Forces. When a man attested (volunteered) under the Group Scheme he was not immediately called up and during this interim period he was allowed to wear an armlet showing that he had volunteered and therefore avoid the stigma of being thought of as a 'slacker' or 'shirker'.

29 January

Coley in the evening to see Dr Jowett with reference to Will, who will have to appeal again to the Tribunal. Called to see the Miss Greenwood, came here by train. Cars are too crowded at night to be comfortable.

30 January

Moderate day. Will & Ma ran up to Todmorden.

31 January

SS Appam which was thought sunk has been taken to Virginia in charge of prize crew.

The SS *Appam* had been captured by the German raider SMS *Mowe* and sent to America with a prize crew on board. The British owners successfully took the German government to court and had the ship and cargo returned to them.

1 February

Zeppelin Raid tonight bombs were dropped. Norfolk. Lincolnshire. Leicester Staffordshire & Derbyshire 54 killed & 69 injured this is coming too near to be liked.

2 February

Will went to Oldham today to bring some 20/- singles this is his first transaction let us hope it will lead to his success.

Seize hold of Gods hand & look full in the face of his creation and there is nothing he will not enable you to achieve Ruskin

Robinson Crusoe at the Royal this week but it was only a moderate Co.

3 February

All streets here in darkness, just a small light at the principal corners to show you where you are. Some mills are lit up all night, this shows the one sidedness of things.

Lighting regulations had been introduced in 1915 in an effort to hamper the German Zeppelin raids. There was, however, much confusion with some premises being allowed to show lights and others not.

4 February

Heavy rain today. Bought Old Curiosity Shop today 6d, a marvel of cheapness, good print etc etc.

5 February

Went to spend the weekend with J Walker, Mary. I got there early afternoon, we had most enjoyable evening reading etc etc interspersed with music.

6 February

Wild wet day. Spent the day looking at books etc J W has got a good library, all in well bound volumes. Bertha not so well.

7 February

Wild wet day. No special war news today. This long suspense is terrible. Good staff are still rushing up.

8 February

Sunshine, Snow, Hail, Rain at intervals. Mrs Joe Wood buried today.

9 February

Cold snap this morning. Reading a small volume of poetry by Omar Khayyan

Lo! Some we loved, the loveliest & the best
That time & fate of all their vintage prest
Have drunk their cup a bound or two before
And one by one adapt silently to rest
Better be merry with the fruitful grape
Than sadder after more or bitter fruit
With them the seed of Wisdom did I sow
And with my own hand laboured it to grow
And this was all the harvest that I reap
I came like water & like wind I go
One moment in Annihilations waste
One moment of the well of life to taste
The stars are setting and the Caravan
Starts for the dawn of nothing Oh make haste

Went to West Vale tonight called to see Joe

10 February

Fearful heavy fall of snow & rain, the roads etc etc were very heavy indeed.

11 February

Dr Jowett came this evening to enquire about Will, and having written him he was very anxious to hear how we had gone on with our appeal, he was very pleased when we told him, it was a bitter cold night, & he was far from well so we persuaded him to stay all night.

12 February

Brighter day but very cold. Today paper report loss of one of our cruisers in the North Sea, turned out to be a mine sweeper.

13 February

Miserable cold day. Startling news this morning. All Single Men to be called up by March 18th, so we are in for a depressing few weeks.

The Germans all along the western front these last few days, have been trying to break through but at about every point have been thrown back with heavy losses. Loss of the Cruiser "Arethusa" mined off the East Coast & feared will be a total wreck.

Manchester Chamber of Commerce reject Business with the Bosche, we must protect our industries for the future, protection has built up Germany's Army , Navy & her trade just before the war was running us the tightest race in the world & would soon have overshadowed us in the trade of the world but this war will end this thank God.

Wild wet snowy weather all the week. Economy is paraded in all the papers, women are going in for shorter frocks.

Germans have taken some of our trenches, they have made strenuous efforts this last few days, but this is only temporary

I suppose.

17 February

(Miss Jowetts Birthday). Turks great fortress of Erzerum captured. The Sultans chief asiatic citadel. Just victory for the Grand duke with great number of guns & large quantity of ammunition & thousand of prisoners.

18 February

Nothing but this everlasting rain

Necessity is always cruel

(The Garden of Lies)

Flour touched 51/- per sack at Liverpool from 27/- before the war

19 February

Rather better day. Stayed at home no amusements no nothing, these are not times for those stayed at home, & to relieve my mind got a good book from the library "Garden of Lies".

Waterloo Cup

M E Hulton Owner Harmonicon the Cup Winner with Hopsack the defeated dog

Don't look for flaws as you go through life

And even when you find them

It is wiser and kind to be somewhat blind

And look for solace behind them

20 February

Very quiet day.

21 February

Colne Valley Harriers here today, I hear they had a good day turned up 4 or 5 hares, but it was dull & foggy, if I could have just had a few hours I should have been delighted, its fine sport.

22 February

Mr Asquith told the House today that the War was costing £4,400,000 a day. Think of this for one moment & it takes your breath. A German Gun came to Halifax today for exhibition it was captured at Loos.

23 February

This I think the coldest day of the winter freezes your marrow. Our aircraft have been doing splendid work this week 26 went up altogether & did a fearful amount of damage.

The streets & houses just near here in total darkness, makes it bad at night for getting about. But then I remember when we had no gas lights in the streets, or houses for that matter, we used to use lanterns when we went out at dark and we lived through these times, and they were happy, better than the times we are having now.

Will sold his Motor Cycle & Sidecar today, coming events look very black, he might be called up, & if not cannot ride it openly in the street, so we all feel the loss, it has been our only source of enjoyment for some time.

24 February

Germans are making great effort on Verdun against the French but I think it will be a failure, in all their attacks their losses are fearful.

The Germans attacked Verdun in an attempt to destroy the French army. It turned into a slogging match in which they suffered almost as much as the French.

25 February

Heavy fall of snow again during the night according to the papers it is very general. Five day heavy attack by a huge German Army on Verdun, but they have made little progress but of heavy loss.

26 February

The Country from Lands End to the North in the grip of winter, heavy snow some villages isolated in the north of Yorkshire.

Lines written in a long case clock

Could but our tempers move, like this machine

Not urged by passion, or delayed by spleen

And true to Natures regulating power

By virtues acts distinguished every hour

Then health & joy would follow as the night

The laws of motion & the laws of thought

Sweet health to pass the present moments over

And every lasting joy when time shall be no more

27 February

Could not go out today roads etc almost knee deep in snow broth.

Great attack on the French on Verdun but the Germans have had appalling losses & little gains.

28 February

Another P&O boat sunk by mine and several others, these losses are terrible. Rather better day. Will went to Stockport to pull down the Cheese Winding Frame.

29 February

The Verdun struggle still rages, the French have trapped them, 45,000 Germans killed, losses phenomenal, the Germans are appalled at the slaughter. Cheese Winding Frame came today by motor wagon, got it in alright.

1 March

Thus ends wild wet Feb. Now we may expect March winds. If it's anything I don't like its high winds, I am frightened. Weather still cold.

2 March

Verdun Battle still rages but up to date the Germans have made no headway and at frightful losses. Snow & sleet almost all the week.

3 March

West Vale tonight called to see Joe, the war does not affect him, as usual full of fun. Bought Rameackers Cartoons for 2d, he is a genius & has nailed the Kaiser to a cross of immortal infamy.

4 March

M J & myself went to Coley in the evening to see Dr Jowett came home by the train. Snow & rain.

5 March

M J went to Todmorden at noon. J Noble came on in the evening. Tonight we had a scare about 10.30 we were roused by the buzzer to warn us that Zeppelins were coming this way, trams were stopped, gas turned off, so for the first time we realised the terrors of war, we were terribly upset & stayed up late but none came thank God.

6 March

Another nerve straining day & this has been going on since Dec. I went to appeal this afternoon at the local Tribunal for Will, he went with me. I think by the questions they asked us etc. our appeal will be favourable, but shall know tomorrow.

Another Zeppelin raid, 8 counties visited, 3 in number were seen, reports give 12 killed & 33 injured, and several houses destroyed, but I am afraid more casualties will be known tomorrow.

7 March

Will's paper came this morning. he has been put back till the 1st September, this is a great relief, the strain has been awful. Let us hope the war will be settled before then.

Snow & sleet for several week now, this has become almost intolerable, my poor feet have been put to a severe test. Very heavy fall of snow, the hills around here are almost impassable, north Yorkshire have had terrible fall of snow & fearful loss of cattle & sheep.

9 March

The fight for Verdun has been a fearful loss of life for the Germans. Mr & Mrs Ernest Rothwell came down this evening stayed supper, we had an enjoyable hour or two, the night was bad so they took the Taxi.

10 March

More trouble today with one of our twiners. Packed up & left us without any notice. Put £2000 Insurance on for Zeps.

11 March

Dull day with showers of sleet. We worked rather late getting things straight then made for home to the fireside & thankful for that.

Much discussion has gone on about some of our troops seeing Angels at "Mons". Reading Modern Painters by Ruskin this passage occurs,

'If some people see Angels when others see only empty spaces let them paint the angels'

There were no angels at the Battle of Mons in 1914. A journalist wrote a fictional account of the battle which involved bowmen from Agincourt coming to the aid of the British army. The story was seized upon as a factual account, in spite of the strenuous denials of the author, and the legend was born.

12 March

Miserable day, snow & sleet, we all stayed at home, in fact we were afraid to leave the fireside

13 March

The tribunals are very busy, every day sees some of our friends having to join. Ma went to Halifax to have her eyes tested for new frames.

14 March

The weather is cruel, for weeks we have simply waded through snow & rain & today has taken the biscuit.

15 March

No war news today. Wet again today, and cold.

Burn's letter sold for £225. A letter written by Burns to Mrs Dunlop in 1788 was sold at Sotherby's yesterday for £225. The letter contains the famous confession of his private marriage to Jean Armour.

16 March

Today we had a most agreeable change the sun broke out in the morning and for an hour or two was lovely it felt we were honoured by his presence.

17 March

Busy day.

18 March

Mill working this afternoon until 5 o'clock. Will went to spend the weekend at Oldham. M J and myself went to Huddersfield in the evening. The town was crowded, and all in darkness, so we did not stay long.

Tried to get to the Theatre but the place packed.

19 March

Dull heavy day, we had a restful day. We went to the Parish Church Evening, Canon Winter preached an excellent service.

20 March

Cold day out. Air raid on Kent considerable damage done to property many killed & wounded.

21 March

The German attacks at Verdun are repulsed every time, the French confident of their success. Allied aircraft did considerable damage to Zebrugge yesterday. West Vale tonight.

22 March

Cold day with a light fall of snow. Rumour of a Naval Engagement in North Sea, but no public statement yet. Bert Law at Tribunal today lost his appeal & will be called up May 1st.

23 March

Naval engagement in the North Sea but news scrappy, we shall hear later on.

24 March

Very busy today, we are short handed and we had heavy deliveries to get away etc. and wage day as well & working all the week until 7 o'clock. Keeps us going at top speed.

25 March

Morning at the mill today while 3 o'clock, this has been a very hard week. M J went to Hipperholme, it turned out a very wild wet night.

26 March

Snow is again with us this morning. M J went to Todmorden. Gilbert Robinson came in afternoon.

27 March

Bitter cold snap today. Nothing new from the front but the German submarines have been very active this last few days and have sunk many ships.

28 March

Bitter cold N wind today the coldest day I think we have had.

29 March

Mrs Eastwood & Hilda came on this evening. The March Lamb came in pretty stiff but it went out this year Frozen Mutton.

30 March

Weather looking better, the sun broke out today & made things look brighter, the long days of rain & snow makes us thankful for sunshine.

31 March

French are still holding the Germans at Verdun, this failure on the part of Germans is the beginning of the end. Zeppelin raid again tonight on the south east coast, 4 or 5 took part much damage was done & loss of life but we managed for the first time to bring one Zeppelin down at the estuary of the Thames & captured the crew, but unfortunately it was sunk.

1 April

Went to Huddersfield with Will to the Theatre to see "Betty" very good.

2 April

M J went to Todmorden by noon train. Another Zeppelin raid on the N E coast of Scotland & considerable damage was done, this is becoming a serious menace.

3 April

Zeppelin Raid again at Hull many killed & considerable damage to property.

4 April

Today news tells of the French trapping Germans round Verdun, they melted away, the French have fought valiantly here & are over confident that they will drive them back, this is the worst blow they have suffered and at frightful losses never to be calculated.

5 April

Merchant shipping of many nationalities have been sunk during the week.

To watch the corn grow and blossom set, to draw hard breath over ploughshare and spade, to think, to love, to hope to pray. These are the things to make man happy.

James Briggs died in America, son of Walter Briggs of Greetland. he enlisted at 17 years of age & went thru the Crimea War. Alma, Inkerman & Sebastapol, he went to America 40 years ago I remember him very well.

6 April

Brighter weather, but still bitter cold out of the sun. Budget this year somewhat staggers us. Income, Matches, Amusements, Railway Tickets, Sugar, Mineral Water. Motor cars & Motor Cycles etc etc.

7 April

Busy day always now with wages & working overtime run us very hard, keeping up with the heavy work it entails. As usual John Bull getting his hand down.

Bought Dickens stories I have long wanted that most delightful story "Boots", Holly Tree Inn but could not tell which of the books it was in, but I would not be put off any longer so called at W H Smiths Shop in Huddersfield & they found it for me I was delighted.

8 April

Lieut Harvey Street came to spend the weekend with us, he came from Clipstone Camp. We all went to Huddersfield in the evening, looked in at Earnshaw's saw a beautiful Indian motorcycle, all taken with it.

9 April

To tea today we had both Lieut Street & Lieut Walker an Elland friend of ours, they are both in the same camp, how strange. Harvey left at 9.30 night to go to Clipstone, he leaves there next week for Birmingham.

10 April

Fine clear day. Register of Motor Cycle. 1408 Miles.

£80

11 April

Will went to Bradford tonight to look at an Indian Motor Cycle 1915 model, not been ridden much & without a scratch, he was wild about it. He bought it straight away the gentleman who had owned it had got a 2 seater car, he told Will that he had the best bargain in Yorkshire. He said it was a gem

& was sorry to part with it. Joss went with him they got back after 10 o clock. In going home Joss had a bad spill, his sidecar came off, but he luckily escaped a nasty accident, we were pleased not worse only a buckled wheel.

12 April

Rainy day. Will on pins all day, he is delighted but managed to get out & try his new mount of course he is delighted & so are we. It is a most beautiful machine & I hope we shall have good luck with it.

13 April

Cold wind. Called at the Bank with Will to sign book etc etc and make the firm now Wm H Stott & Son this ought to have been done earlier, he now practically runs the place.

14 April

Bitter cold shivery day, rain & snow. Very heavy day at the mill, heavy deliveries of yarn came in & this makes it very hard work, but I suppose we must be thankful.

15 April

Will took his Mother to Bradford on the new bike, she is afraid it is too fast. Flag day at Elland, "Cruelty to Children". Raised £74.

16 April

Miserable day.

17 April

Heavy showers at intervals. No fresh news from the front of any importance. America have again sent a note to Germany about sinking her ships, this time it has to be final if it happens so but I expect she will funk again.

18 April

Will went to Rochdale today on his machine to see F Smith, it turned out a wet journey.

19 April

Russians notable success 50,000 prisoners. Walk round Tag Lock this morning cold raw morning, vegetation backward. Coltsfoot was the only flower in bloom. I never heard any of the migrants or saw swallows, there seems a little colony of gulls settled in the flat there close to the Sewerage Works. For a few years they have come here. I watched them fly about with their graceful sweeps, Peewits are here as well. I crossed the Calder by the new bridge & got into the main road, a few days ago there was a heavy land slide close to the Rawsons Arms, part of the hill came right onto the road, and in one place brought a large tree with it. I suppose the heavy wet weather of the last month has been the cause, and as one man remarked the heavy motor traffic now terribly shakes the ground. The walk round there is very pleasant.

The Russian success noted by William was the Lake Naroch offensive. It was in fact a failure with heavy Russian casualties.

He who walks humbly with nature will seldom be in danger of losing sight of Art.
Ruskin

Reading "The God of Love" by Justin McCarthy a capital story founded on Dante & Beatrice must have something to read to take this dreadful nightmare off our minds.

20 April

Heavy day at mill, delivery of skips came that fast that we cannot keep up with them and its all sheer muscle work handling them.

21 April (Good Friday)

No playing this year at all, everybody busy with being short handed.

22 April

Now for a few days out thank God, I was off soon as possible to Todmorden to J Walters got there about 4 o'clock after tea we went into the town, it was the Fair, then home to our books etc. M J & Will were going to Bradford on the machine.

23 April (Easter Day)

Bright morning M J & Will came up before dinner then Will went forward to Oldham to see Harvey, he stayed all night but I think he got fed up.

24 April (Easter)

Wet morning. Stayed indoors all day, J W has a splendid collection of books & we both had a good read & chat about them. He gave me an excellent volume, Dickens "Bleak House".

25 April

Will came from Oldham He then went to Halifax Barracks with Uncle John to see Capt Moorhouse about him being called to the colours on Saturday. It was a good thing he did go or he might have been fetched.

26 April

Put in a new Appeal this morning first thing, we were in an awful dilemma M J as usual was flying from one point of the compass to the other, jotting every detail of information possible. While here I have been reading a capital book "Panama, and what it means" by Foster Fraser a capital work on this subject. The book really belongs to J A Ingham who very strange to say owns an island, The island of St Jose close to the entrance of the canal on the Pacific side of the Isthmus and now he thinks it will be required as a coaling station for the canal. He has just got damages in a law suit at San Francisco over this purchase. The book tell in a graphic manner how this huge undertaking has been accomplished & how they have had to fight the fever laden country but they have succeeded by destroying the mosquitoes which have laid thousands of lives when the French attempted to cut the canal, he sums up the book as follows. Accordingly on even terms British Shipping with the east & with Australia has nothing to gain by Panama.

Sinn Feiners rising in Ireland, and of a serious aspect, armed body of men seized several important houses in the City of Dublin, Germans have been supplying them with arms, a disguised ship was captured, with some, also Sir Roger Casement was captured, this rebel it seems has been in the pay of the Germans, but he will be tried for treason & shot I hope. 67 days of siege at Verdun still leave the French masters of the situation.

At this time the whole of Ireland was part of Great Britain. On 24 April the Irish Republicans launched an uprising, mainly in Dublin, to end British rule and establish an independent Irish Republic. The British army quickly brought in reinforcements including artillery and on 29 April the Republicans surrendered unconditionally.

28 April

Will had a busy day again, had to go to the Barracks again, but we are somewhat more settled, as he will have to await his appeal, if they don't put him back to his tribunal decision Sept 1st. I think they will. M Jane Birthday.

29 April

Gen Townsend surrenders Kut, failures of supplies, his force consisted of 9000 British troops of whom 2/3 were Indian troops & their followers.

The fall of Kut, in present day Iraq, was a major blow to the British Mesopotamian campaign. The siege lasted from December 1915 until 29 April 1916 with 23,000 British and Indian soldiers dying in attempts to relieve the garrison.

What with the Rebellion in Ireland, use of the Post Office etc etc serious riots many killed & wounded Martial Law prevails. Troops ordered out there, it looks like the end of the world, also loss of ships daily make us all begin to think the bitterness of our struggle

30 April

Fine day I went to Todmorden afternoon with Will on new Indian it runs very well, found them all very well got home about 8 o'clock.

1 May

Revolt in Ireland subsiding but the damage estimated at 3 Millions. Sackville St the pride of Dublin a heap of ruins, 3 of the ring leaders were found by Court Martial guilty & were shot this morning.

2 May

General Compulsion for Service expected to be brought in tomorrow, so evidently the Government are getting every available man and boy by the end of this terrible war. F R Benson the well known Shakesperian Actor & for a long number of years has kept always a capital Co together playing nothing else but Shakespeare all over England, and his school has produced some of our best actors. Last night the King called him to the Royal Box after playing "Julius Caesar" & Knighted him on the spot, this very gratifying to me and all lovers of Shakespeare.

Compulsion Bill brought in, youths of 18 to enlist & married men up to 41. This now looks serious business & the darkest look out of our time.

4 May

Very distressing cases of young men now daily being called up to the colours, we are living in daily dread over our dear boy, and we are doing our best at his next appeal on which looks very very critical.

5 May

90th Birthday of Empress Eugenie may she live to see Alsace & Lorraine taken back to her dear France.

Empress Eugenie was the last Empress of France. She, along with her husband, was deposed in 1870 and lived in exile in England until her death in 1920.

6 May

Cold bitter day for May. German reply to America still unsatisfactory, simply evading the questions.

7 May

St Johns Anniversary. M J & myself went Evening Service Rev J H Walker was the preacher and we were deeply interested in his sermon. Lack of parental control, allowing children to grow up in their own wilful way was sure to bring trouble to the child & disaster to the nation. The choir sang the Anthem "Praise the Lord" in a very praise worthy manner, I don't suppose we have missed an anniversary here & all our old friends gave us a hearty welcome, but they are becoming less.

9 May

Another trial today. We had to make further appeal at the Elland Tribunal tonight, and we are all doubtful about the result, we await the decision with great trouble, what will become of the mill without his help God alone knows.

10 May

After an anxious night, M J did not sleep, we received by post the news that Will was put back till 1st Sept so we were relieved another time. Another heavy attack on Verdun & the loss of Germans is said to be 60,000. The estimated loss up to date for Germany is over 2 Million.

11 May

Drill Hall Halifax. Miss Mabel Jowett was giving a Patriotic Concert she had trained the School Children. Story of Prince Charles, Flora McDonald, and they played it exceedingly well it was under the patronage of the Officers of the Barracks & they were in full force. Dr Jowett was in military uniform as Chaplain & he strutted about like a youth.

12 May

Dull showery day but much warmer. Potatoes are ½ per lb. Germans are exhausted at Verdun.

13 May

Very cold and showery. Never went out only to change my library. Will a shocking bad cold which has left him very deaf, we are much concerned about it.

"Fossitts Circus" visited Elland today, of course I could not resist, they had a fair show, the usual riding & some very comical clowns.

14 May

York today with Will, Mr Dixon & Mr Murray for companions, left 10.30. Very good run, we went to see the damages done by the Zeps the other day, they were bad done & very considerable amount of damage. Left at 3.30 got home 6.30 it was bitter cold coming back with heavy wind and rain 92 miles.

Reading today I now think the end of the War will not be very long, Germany knows today that she is broken but like the gambler she is playing for the stake, with our rapid strides in munitions both for ourselves and for our allies, the end cannot be long delayed.

17 May

Daylight Bill comes into operation on Sunday. York via Leeds & Tadcaster, the morning was clear but threatening after getting thro Leeds the country is very pretty. We arrived in York 1.30, we asked some native to tell us where we could see where the damage was done & we went to Nunthorpe Road & here we saw an awful sight, the street was half wrecked, not a whole pane of glass whole, windows, doors, slates, chimney pots, some houses completely wrecked & the tenants killed and maimed, 6 were killed, 3 have died since from injuries & 45 in the Hospital. The Airship came on the city with only 10 minutes warning, it hovered over the city for a few minutes, but after dropping the bombs in went back in an E direction, many bombs fell on the Knavesmire without

any damage. The Minster thank God escaped these murderous Huns. Went to West Vale in the evening. Trial of Sir Roger Casement the organiser of the German Sinn Fein movement why a trial he ought to have been shot on the spot the traitor.

18 May

A real summers day this is delightful after our long winter & very cold spring the sudden change made us all languid?

19 May

Glorious summer came at once.

20 May

Brilliant sunshine all day, cannot bear to work in the heat. John Walker & Mary came to spend the weekend with us. J W and myself went to Huddersfield in the evening.

21 May

Daylight Saving Bill came into operation today all clocks were put forward I hour until October, this scheme is supposed to save 2 ½ Millions in coal & gas. I hope it will prove true.

22 May

Will went to Ripon & Harrogate today. Beautiful day. We found everybody at their work this morning despite alterations.

23 May

Desperate fighting still prevails around Verdun with heavy losses to the enemy.

24 May

Grim harvest of the Verdun struggle 19 trains laden with German corpses they are cremating them in Flemish black furnaces. I see in the paper that David E Hirst who formerly lived at Greetland, has returned after 34 years service at Lincoln Cathedral as alto singer.

The Dean on behalf of the members of the Cathedral made him a handsome Cheque, he was also a Violinist & Conductor of many Musical Societies in Lincoln, he was always ready with his help. I am glad of this appreciation he was a member of our first Minstrel Troupe & was a great help he could both play violin & sing etc etc. I called to see him once in Lincoln and was made very welcome.

27 May

Alexander Day. Another flower day, pretty girls swarmed the streets selling the Wild Rose for Infirmary etc, money easily raised in fact nobody feels it. Came in cold & showery in the evening I only went out to change my library, then early bed.

28 May

Salmon & New Potatoes for dinner. M J & Will ran up to Todmorden afternoon. Coley Chapel in the Evening sorry to find Dr Jowett in deep trouble, his Sister died last week after undergoing an operation, called at the Vicarage stayed supper, the garden was in full bloom trees in blossom, but the master hand was gone. Mrs Jowett was never tired with her garden & always had it beautiful, Dr J carefully protects the birds, he showed me many nests.

30 May

Very heavy day & I was not so well, I am worried by many things, I cannot do anything right. 100th day battering at Verdun without any progress, but at fearful losses to the Huns.

31 May

Very cold in the evening. Our Will & Mr Dixon the Chemist are making tests on their Motor machines with a mixture to improve the mileage, after long and careful experiments they get 28% more out of a Gallon of Petrol with this new mixture, this if it holds out will prove a great help now that the spirit is very dear & I hope it will turn out to themselves.

Butter 1/8 & some cases more per lb & milk so thin that it won't run out of the can.

Threatened Strike of Cotton Operatives Lancashire & Yorkshire as if we had not trouble enough on land. Has this war come to settle these labour demons, I think it has.

1 June

Very cold all day the evening was more like October very cold wind, had to put on my overcoat. Pictures House "After Dark" film play G Bracewell very good.

2 June

Naval misfortune. Great excitement was caused tonight by the announcement that our fleet had met with disaster in the North Sea, the cruisers Queen Mary, Indefatigable, Invincible & 8 other ships sunk, this list only to hand I am afraid they have not told us the worst. We are not up in scientific devilry like the Huns. Another loss like this and our Navy will be practically finished.

The battle of Jutland had taken place from 31st May to 1st June. Although the German fleet inflicted more casualties on the British they were forced to retreat back into port and they never ventured out again. Poor safety measures caused the three cruisers named above to explode with heavy loss of life.

4 June

Cold shivery day. More news today unhappily the lives in the lost battle ships exceed the gloomiest forebodings, with one or two exceptions all the officers were killed in action, or went down with their doomed ship, the crews generally doubtless suffered the same fate. Zeppelins are said to have done as much damage to our ships. Later news tells a different story our loss is appalling but the enemy is worse.

The German Heavy Fleet attacked Admiral Beatty Light Fleet, the latter immediately faced the foe at heavy odds expecting Admiral Jellico Fleet coming to his rescue but he was 400 miles further north, but got there at the finish then the Germans turned tail & fled, Jellico

chased them hundreds of miles but could not get at them. They have lost 18 Ships and many damaged, they as usual sent wireless lies to the American Press that their loss was not severe. Lord Beresford says ours is the greatest Victory on record although our losses are heavy.

6 June

Tonight's paper. Greatest disaster of the war. Lord Kitchener and his staff drowned on his way to Russia. HMS Hampshire torpedoed or mined. We have had to endure many heavy blows during the war but the dire news that comes today puts others in the shade. Lord Kitchener & staff have been drowned will stagger the Empire. Through all his career he has accomplished every task he undertook, his great work in Egypt will be a standing monument to his name. But his great work was in organising, his genius was formidable, and never in the worlds history has anyone accomplished a military task so difficult as his call to arms, in one year an army of 5 Million.

"Echo de Paris" pays a striking tribute to Kitcheners Death while doing his duty worthily crowns a career of character almost legendary. His coffin is a warship and the sea his tomb. One imagines his tall figure rising above the waves to watch the battles of the armies he created to crush Germany.

John Dempster of the firm R W Dempster (Gas Plant Manufacturer) died this week, they have risen rapidly & become very wealthy. I knew him well in my salad days & was always pleased to meet him. He was very fond of yachting, on one occasion at Kiel he won a prize & the Kaiser came aboard his yacht to lunch.

Reported this evening one seaman has been landed at Blythe from the ill fated "Hampshire", this was later contradicted. Bitter cold weather.

Whilst en route to Russia on a diplomatic mission, Lord Kitchener, the Secretary of State for War, was drowned when the ship he was travelling in struck a mine and sank.

KITCHENER
JUNE 5TH
"Matt's" Splendid Cartoon
Daily Despatch
CARRY ON
So midst this bitter strife,
We hail with reverent breath,
Our leader, great in life,
And greater still in death.
"Democritus"

8 June

Holidays in a many place will not be observed this year, all Munitions shops are requested to work in fact we all ought to do. Russia are again in great force against German Austrian army taking enormous number of prisoners & guns.

For once the reports were correct. On 6th June the Russians had attacked the Austro-Hungarians and inflicted a major defeat upon them. The offensive continued until September with the Russians advancing a considerable distance.

9 June

Very cold weather indeed for the last few days I have worn my overcoat.

10 June

Stopped for the Holidays some are showing their patriotism by running, our landlord looked to his pocket so we had to play.

11 June

Cold raw showery day. West Vale Church with M J Evening Service. Memorial Service for Kitchener & two lads from West Vale one in the Navy who was killed in the North Sea Battle and the other the army & was killed in action in France. Mrs Richardson spoke exceedingly well. Dead March finished the service.

12 June

Whit. It was bitter cold day. We intended having a spin but dare not face the cold weather, some of the mills were working but majority played. Went walk round Skircoat with J Noble but we were perished with cold.

13 June

Papers this morning tell of fall of snow in many parts. I have never in my time experienced such cold weather at Whitsuntide.

14 June

Miss Lillian Fox daughter of the late David Fox was married at Parish Church Ayr to Mr Alfred Bramhill Doe, this will cause a flutter in the Smithies Dovecotes, if no issue they come in for her fortune so we await with interest results.

You have no doubts about the ability of Admiral Beatty.

AB No we will go to Hell with Beatty.

Russians Advance incessant and victorious "Kovel" threatened this is a most important position, if taken will destroy enemy's most important connections Austrian & German front.

15 June

Bright sunny day but a blizzard of a wind, had to keep overcoats on & keep them well buttoned up too. Ripponden evening on the sidecar saw & spoke to Old Sam Mellor the local poet, he looks very feeble, I asked him about his sketch "Old Oilse" but he not a copy left.

16 June

Russians still forging ahead and taking thousands of prisoners & guns etc. Austria I think will throw in the sponge they seem to have had enough they are not getting the German support they had.

17 June

Haworth this afternoon with Will on the sidecar to the Bronte Centenary (Charlotte), we could not get into church it was packed Bishop Weldon was speaking, we went to the Bronte Museum & were much interested, we came home over Cock Hill a most delightful ride, we lingered long on the hill top. The day was delightful over Cock Hill & down the Hebden Bridge Valley I know no lovelier scenery.

Nature paints for all the world poor/rich together (Ruskin)

Our pilgrimage to Haworth was most enjoyable. I could not let the opportunity pass without showing my appreciation of the Bronte Family, Charlotte of course was the most pronounced but Emily I think was the most poetic some of her poems are beautiful. To think that the quaint old fashioned town of Haworth far from any town and close to the wild bleak moorland should have reared such geniuses that have made their names immortal in our English literature and the tragedy of it was that they all died young. Branwell their only brother who was a blot on the family died at 32. The first time I was at Haworth was at the last service of the Old Church we were shown the marriage certificate in the register there and other things as well. We called at the Black Bull on that occasion & sat in the chair that Branwell Bronte once spent so many hours in this well known house. Today the chair was an exhibition and a charge was made, but the funds were to be given to the Red Cross Fund this was too and enough has been said & written of Branwell, let us be charitable. Let us look at Charlottes letter to her sister a day or two after his death. He is in God's hands now; and the all powerful is likewise the all merciful, a deep conviction that he rests at last-rests well, after his brief erring, suffering, feverish life falls & quits my mind now till the last hour I've never known how much we can forgive. pity, regret a near relative. All his vices are nothing now We remember only his woes. We walked thru the village to the Church yard with the Parsonage in the background, which I expect will be honoured by lovers of literature in generations to come, I feel glad we were present to swell the numbers of the Bronte Society who figured largely in today's proceedings.

18 June

Restful day.

19 June

Bright & sunny but still cold wind. Russians again today are making rapid strides. Austrians are completely sorted.

20 June

British troops I think now are going to take the offensive. Verdun battle losing its force but the Germans still trying but the French repulse them every time.

21 June

Strawberries are here. The longest day today and we have had no warm weather since Sept we have had cold bleak weather and now we are faced with shorter days. Greece climbs down. All the Ententes demands accepted. Petrol to be taxed at 6d per gallon.

The Allies had sent troops into Greece, a neutral country, in the autumn of 1915. This caused an uneasy situation until there was a coup assisted by the French and British which installed a pro-allied government which acquiesced to the allied demands.

22 June

Cool day. Russians pursuit, the enemy vacating Lemberg. Verdun still holding the Germans in check & at heavy loss.

23 June

Beautiful weather.

24 June

Thunder shower this afternoon. Huddersfield in the morning with the advent of cars we can either go to Huddersfield or Halifax same price. The town was very busy walked round the shops then came home.

25 June

Beautiful day. Our folks went to Todmorden. Today papers tell of heavy fighting around Verdun, they are making every effort to break through, I hope they will frustrated.

26 June

Today's news tell us of the combined attack of the Allies on the west & heavy fighting has taken place.

27 - 29 June

Will & Mr Dixon have for a considerable time been experimenting with a Petrol Saver, it is a powder they have thought out and after exhaustive trials find they can get 28% more mileage with this mixture added to the Petrol. They have got it now on the market "Petriox" and I think it will be a success seeing that the price of Petrol is so very expensive. The Russians have driven Austrians into Romania territory & have been disarmed.

Irvine Holt called to see us, he is looking very well, he is stationed in County Cork in a Convalescent Camp but doing clerical work just now, he has had 9 months and never out of shell range so I think he has done his bit.

30 June

Reading Agnes Grey by Annie Bronte

John Cornwall the 16 year old boy of whom Admiral Beatty wrote I recommend his case for special recognition, mortally wounded he remained at his post waiting orders until the battle was over.

1 July

Very cold chilly day. The great push British & French are taking the offensive on a 90 mile front & are driving the Huns back.

The long awaited Somme offensive had started. It was the first major action of Kitchener's New Army of volunteers. It got off to a very bad start with 20,000 men killed on the first day although the press were optimistic in their reports.

2 July

Brighter day. This morning brings better news from the front, great advance.

3 July

The day goes well for England & France.   (Reuters Message)

4 July

Advances all along the line, Germans driven out of the trenches.

5 July

Capture of thousands of Germans, our Artillery is playing havoc just now, we have just got to the point the Huns had when the war started but now we are better equipped than they are at present.

All Allied Counties are determined to close the door to this monster and about time. He would have beaten us without fighting for it, in another 10 years of trade. he had got practically hold of the lot.

Tonight Mr Farrar & Mr Thomas, motor enthusiasts, called, Walter Greenwood also there we had a long sitting & of course talked about nothing but Motors etc etc.

Scenes at Manx Ceremony at Tynwald Hill, the inhabitants of the island are much dissatisfied at the absence of the Governor of the Isle of Man, Lord Raglan for a period of 8 months when the island is in such distress owing to no visitors going since the war started. He received a very horrible demonstration, one woman knocked his hat off with a sod.

6 July

Today the news is very cheering. French capture 76 Guns & hundreds of machine guns. Germans seem demoralised by British Artillery, we also captured thousands of Germans. The Russians are battling heroically.

7 July

Our casualties in the last push have been very heavy, but our success great. Farmers just now have their grass cut but owing to the rain are unable to get it housed.

8 July

Another Birthday passed.

Cool day but the evening turned out very fine I walked up to see Mr Rothwell. M J went to Hipperholme to see Misses Greenwood.

Another flower day, this for the sailors & National Lifeboat Institution. British & French on the offensive on a long front and successful but the casualties are heavy the papers are full of portraits of the fallen.

9 – 12 July

Missing from diary.

13 July

Rather better weather but it will require a lot of thinking that its summer time. Farmers have plenty of grass but cannot harvest it.

14 July

Tonight news we have broken into the 2nd Trenches & gained a few miles, taken many guns and prisoners.

15 July

British Great Push. The last few days have seen severe fighting but we had achieved great success, gaining ground & taken a large number of prisoners & guns. Miss Greenwood came to tea this afternoon our Bertha came as well. Meat so dear that last week we bought a small ham, it was nice for a change, but to go on day after day I feel ashamed to look a pig in the face.

16 July

Cold & showery. Bertha went home in the evening.

17 July

News today shows what the British Army can do when we have got material to go on with, this last few days we have pushed the enemy 8 miles, got into their 3 trenches & inflicted horrible havoc on the enemy, our new army has decimated their crack Regiment, the Prussian Guard, this has caused great consternation in Germany.

18 July

Received a letter today from Harvey he tells us he is in the trenches, we are much concerned about him, & hope he will have good luck he is very cheerful, but he says the sights are horrible but thinks it will soon be over, let us hope so.

19 July

West Vale tonight saw Joseph Fox who now resides at Rotherham with his daughter, he tells me he is 81 years of age, he had been to Greetland Church this afternoon as he said to look at all his old friends. He thinks he will be the last, he was Organist here for 33 years, I was a choir boy also for a long number of years. He was a very clever man at his business and he assisted my father in the making of all his models for Sewer

Ventilation etc both of Sewers & Skips and they were works of art & reflected great credit on him. We went to the Shears & had a long talk about the old times, he was very interesting I was glad to see him.

Desperate fighting this last few days but we are getting the overhand now and the Germans now know that British when he is equipped he will fight to the bitter end, as to when It will end nobody knows but the stress to me is terrible, the loss of all this young blood will be heavy for the country to bear.

21 July

Splendid day looks like hotting up. Reading "The other Sara" by Curtis Yorke it takes the dumps out of one to read. My first trip on the "Indian".

22 July

Bright sunny day Will took me to Blackpool this afternoon, left about 2.30 delayed a time at Burnley with broken chain after that we spun along very well but the traffic was heavy between Preston & Blackpool, the town was very busy stayed with Mrs Robinson.

Idea of a socialist. Is someone as wants to have nothing to do, and plenty of time to do it in, and plenty of money for doing it.

23 July

Brilliant sunshine, almost intolerable. Called on J W & Mary, Jimmy & Maggie, after dinner we started back, the weather was delightful met Joe & his wife. Called at Whalley here is a large Military Hospital & we saw hundreds of poor wounded soldiers, we then went up the Hodder Valley called to look at Mitton Church with its historical Monuments and Chained Bible then further on to Hodder

Bridge. The river here is lovely & the trees all in their best made it a picture we shall long remember you cannot go wrong here its simply fairyland. Came back to Whalley looking at Stonyhurst College by the way then made for home it was a good run without any stoppages arriving home 6.30.

26 July

Pozieres Captured, signal British success. Very hot weather. Our Bertha sent us a wagon load of coal today so we were busy, we shall be alright next winter thank God. This last few days have seen some heavy fighting. Pozieres now in our possession, this has been a prominent hill which the enemy have long held possession of and of great advantage to them.

27 July

The Russians are forging ahead, this morning paper announces 6000 prisoners thus completing the conquest of Armenia.

28 July

More trouble today at the mill. Tom Midgley, twiner, gave his notice and now refuses to do his work so shall stop him tomorrow.

29 July

Huddersfield this evening Patriotic trade procession, the best I ever saw. Thousands lined the streets & some beautiful tableaux and some very comic ones, thousands lined the street the proceeds were for the Sailors Fund so it would be a good one.

30 July

Beautiful day I never went out of the house.

2 August

"Warp Heads" Annual Outing to Malham via Skipton we started 9 o'clock, arriving at Malham 12 o'clock, dinner at the Roebuck Hotel, after that some went to Gordale Scar & others to Janet's Foss, which was much admired, we spent the time leisurely until 4 o'clock, then boarded the Motor Charabanc to that delightful place Burnsall, and today it was at its best, a capital tea was given us at the Red Lion, we went into the Grammar School, it was here that Eugene Aram was teacher for a time. The lady here has a most beautiful garden & an enthusiast on roses & the garden was one mass of bloom many of our members bought bouquets to bring home, the proceeds the lady gave to the Soldiers Fund. Leaving here we drove to Ilkley & Burley in Wharfedale this is a very pretty place then forward thro Bradford, Hx and home, we arrived here about 10.30, after a most enjoyable day the weather was all that could be desired, & everything passed off without a hitch.

3 August

Casement the Irish Rebel was hanged today. Third Zeppelin raid this week but not much damage.

4 August

Two years today war was declared and according to Mr Balfour we are in a better position than we were at the beginning, we are prepared now, France I see today are loud in praise of England, but for us the Huns would have run roughshod over Europe but he reckoned without his host

Patriotic Sale at Elland raised £183. a Donkey was sold for £63, 4 kittens fetched £4.

6 August

Will took his mother to Harrogate, Knaresbro & home by way of Blubberhouse Moor, a very wild weird place but very pleasant run. I went with some friends to Kirkheaton had a look round this very pretty Church, got home 9.30. Very hot day.

9 August

Mrs Eastwood & Miss Halliday to tea, it is a few years since the latter was here, she is Matron at the Waterloo Hospital London, she was looking very well indeed & we were delighted to have the pleasure of her company, old friends are always welcome.

10 August

Under Gen Cadorna the Italian Army have smashed the Austrians & driven them back in great disorder. The Russians in the East have forged ahead. More Zeppelin raids on the E coast and as far as Scotland, but not a great amount of damage done, a few innocent women & children have had to suffer.

11 August

Russians on the outskirts of Stanislau. Search light on Southowram hill can be seen almost every night. Norland Moor will soon be fitted up with the same.

12 August

Halifax in the afternoon, called at West Vale coming home to see Mrs Eastwood it was her birthday, her brother Alfred was there & we had a long chat, years since I saw him before. Our total national indebtedness at the end of the financial year will be £3,440,000,000 a figure no chancellor of the exchequer has ever had to contemplate before but Mr McKenna is quite unperturbed.

13 August

Will went with Bert Law to Boroughbridge they had a good run. We went to see Mr & Mrs Rothwell, coming home the searchlight on Norland Moor was at work, also Huddersfield and they almost met.

14 August

Stayed about home, weather unsettled. Good progress made E & W at the front.

15 August

Weather showery.

16 August

Morecambe this morning, left by the 8 train to see my old friend Mr William Maud. I heard he was not so well but glad to find him better, they were both pleased (Mr & Mrs) to see me & made me quite happy. He took me up into his studio & for an hour or so, he showed me scores of pictures in various stages of painting so very beautiful things, and he gave me a couple of pictures, landscapes & sea pieces, which will be a good addition to many more of his pictures, of which I have a deep admiration for. We looked also at many of the old favourite pictures which adorned his room, which bring back very happy recollections. I stayed tea with them and then they came to see me off at the station, got home 10.30 *having spent a very happy day with my artistic friend.*

Showery. Finished my Annual Warphead Sketch, got it copied today on postcards, Turned out very well.

17 August

Stayed about home all day the weather was fitful, & the town was very quiet all away at the seaside, I am afraid the weather will have interfered with the pleasure, what a pity after this beautiful weather.

18 August

Afternoon I went to Todmorden to John Walters for the weekend. Steady progress from the read of war in tonight paper.

19 August

Went down Todmorden in the afternoon for a walk with J W. Reading (Ordeal of Silence) by Peer and a very good one.

20 August

Stayed indoors all day reading etc came home by the last train.

21 August

Fight in the North Sea again, we have lost 2 Cruisers, & sunk 2 submarines, this is all the news to hand yet. Today at 2.30 we heard a violent explosion, the shocks were very distinct & dense smoke was visible over the hills we were afraid it was Hipperholme Munitions Works, but later we heard it was Low Moor Munitions Work I am afraid the loss of life will be very heavy. The works were wrecked, & all the houses were shattered, not a whole pane of glass in Low Moor. The place looks horrible. Will ran over on his machine but could not get anywhere near, it was the largest works in England, it will be a national loss.

I shall pass thru this world but once - any good that I can do or any kindness I can show to any fellow creature let me do it now - for I may not pass this way again.

Mrs & Miss Walker called to see us. Ted Buckley came today to spend the week end. Will went to the appeal Committee for Fred Rawnsley, he was refused.

24 August

Widespread regret will be aroused by the death of Mr Ehud Hanson, a genial personality & a good favourite with the public, he was a gifted amateur vocal entertainer, I met

him many times on the platform at our Concerts at West Vale etc He might have made a name & a fortune if he had gone on the stage, he was approached many times but he preferred to give his services for charitable institutions. Russell he acted to a fault. he will be missed, many happy hours I have spent in his charming company in days gone by R.I.P.

27 August

Attended the funeral of Ehud Hanson at Halifax, a very pathetic scene was a number of blind people there, he was ever ready at all Concerts promoted for the Blind, and they paid their last respects.

28 August

Will & Ted went to Buxton with some friends they had a very nice run got home by 9 o'clock.

29 August

Italy & Romania proclaim war, the former on Germany the latter against Austria.

M J went to Halifax to see Mr Edgar Brearley to write out Will's appeal papers, he is in a Solicitors Office in Hx & they are well up on these matters, and he has been exceptionally kind to us on former appeals, we are terribly anxious as almost all single men are now been called up. Fred Rawnsley one of our turners called up for the 11th Sept.

30 August

Up early this morning M J & myself went to Rastrick to interview the Military Representative Hugh Travers Clay and explain our situation & give him facts of our present position as to our appeal next week, he was very kind & listened to all our positions and I think he will put it favourably to the members of the Tribunal, he gave us much encouragement by saying don't worry, but we are all run down with these anxious months that have been hanging over our heads, and besides that our very heavy work at the mill owing to shorthanded, is weighing very heavily on us all, we cannot stand this strain much longer. Germany receives a rude shock now Romania thrown in with the Allies & has started earnest to fight the Austrians.

31 August

Thank God the end looks in sight now. My "Warphead" postcard when printed turned out very well & my friends appreciate it.

1 September

Halifax tonight to the New Picture House to see the film now showing, the Battle of Somme showing sights of the battlefield. Base Hospital, some of the pictures were terrible to look at, the horrors of war are truly represented, I came away with a heavy heart.

This film shot, by Geoffrey Malins and John McDowell, was the first ever war documentary and the scenes shown, although very tame by the standards of today, shocked audiences.

2 September

Greece in revolt, the country want to join the allied power, but the King is the cats paw of the Kaiser, but he would either fight or lose his crown. Afternoon I went to All Saints Church to the opening of the New Organ, Mr Burns gave a Recital some of the tunes were very impressive. Reading "Wayward Ann" by Curtis Yorke, if my mind could not be connected to something else I should go mad, thanks goodness we can have a good book.

3 September

13 Zeppelins_made a raid in the south E coast, one 8 miles north of London was brought down by the aircraft guns, it took fire & came to earth a burning mass, all the men were burned to death, great excitement 15 casualties, and slight damage to property. Intense fighting on the "Somme" with heavy losses to the enemy.

6 September

Will took his Ma to Oldham to see Mr & Mrs Street but they were away. Harvey glad to say has got back to Manchester Whitworth Park Hospital & doing well, we are all so pleased. West Vale tonight called at Joe's, we were in the office, forgetting that the window had no blind the policeman came in, I am afraid poor Joe will be summonsed for they are very strict just now.

Harvey Street was William's cousin. He had been invalided home from the Somme battlefront with trench fever and shell shock.

7 September

Many local men in the last push sorry to say have fallen.

8 September

The Germans are now realising a terrible shock, the heavy bombardments of the British & French Artillery have staggered them.

Lt W L Robinson, the airman who brought down the Zeppelin, is only 21 years of age, it was a daring feat. He was up 2 hours and he had prayed he might have a chance and he got it, he deserves all honour and the British public will give it to him.

Hindenburg has arrived to take charge of the army to arrest the Allies progress.

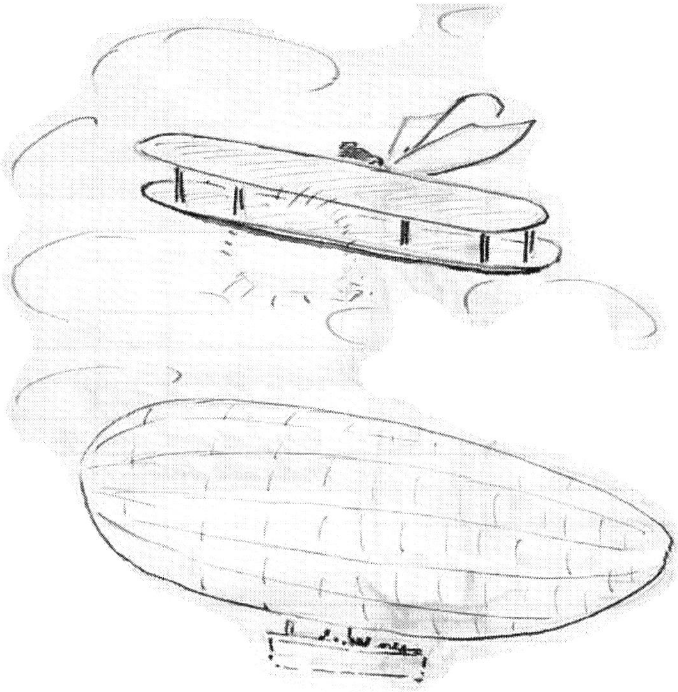

9 September

Nothing to say of any note, so rested, but unfortunately I am getting to that age when rest does not give the relief it used to do. Halifax Hospital very full just now of wounded soldiers.

10 September

We all went to Todmorden afternoon in the sidecar, I rode on the carrier and on this machine it was comfortable, not like the "Rex".

11 September

Another nerve trying ordeal tonight. Appeal tonight for Will at the Tribunal, pleased to say he was put back until January 1st, this to us is a great relief.

12 September

Great forward movement by the French today 3rd line of trenches taken at all points good progress is being made.

13 September

All goes well with us at the front. Had a cheque returned today F & Co.

14 September

Busy day & very unpleasant had some rather bad work in this week & work people complain so had to sweeten them to keep quiet.

15 September

Mary & J Walker came to Greetland this afternoon with M J to the Opening of the New School "St Thomas'". Mrs Arthur Law wired us to meet her at West Vale after the ceremony we all went back to Halifax & spent the evening at Salterville.

17 September

Afternoon with a few friends to Sowerby to look thru the garden of James Farrer the Cactus Expert, he has the largest collection of Cactuses in Yorkshire, we were shown all thro, and I must confess they were really beautiful, many were in full bloom, we saw species from all parts of the globe. Strange to say Mr F is an illiterate man, but he has a worldwide reputation in this line, & could give the scientific names of every specimen he had etc I was delighted by the beautiful plants the like I had never seen before.

19 September

The sad news comes to hand that Raymond Asquith son of the Prime Minister had been killed, he was a brilliant son of a brilliant Father R.I.P.

This afternoon I saw an aeroplane flying N E it came back later on flew over Elland towards Huddersfield, it caused quite a sensation.

20 September

Cold morning now. Severe fighting on the Somme front. Germans pushed 40,000 men against the French, but were repulsed with heavy losses. King of Greece looks like getting help from his Government.

21 September

Armoured cars have been very useful in the last great push, have done fearful destruction they are simply travelling fortress & spread death & destruction all round.

22 September

News of heavy fighting. Norman Farrar called tonight, he lost his appeal, we are all so sorry.

23 September

Afternoon with Will round *<u>Bradford Low Moor</u>* *saw the effects of the explosion a few weeks back, the place looks like there has been an earthquake, home by Queensbury.*

24 September

Will took Ma to Oldham this afternoon to see Harvey, they found him very well but his nerves shattered somewhat.

25 September

Zeppelin raid again yesterday. 12 or 14 visited the S. E. Coast & London, many casualties & properties destroyed. 2 of the Zeps were brought down, one was put on fire, the other the crew were taken prisoners.

26 September

Last night we had an alarm that Zeppelins were coming, reports this morning are very scant, but the E counties have been visited & some parts of Lancashire so reports say this is getting near, Sheffield & Bolton were done much damage.

27 September

The nights now are very dark, no lamps lit & all shops & houses have darkened blinds, make it dangerous to be out at night, & such appearances we have a black winter to look forward to. Beautiful weather.

28 September

The capture of Combles. This has been a strong fortified position, & the Germans thought it almost impossible but the French & British have gained a great victory, at the finish it was described as a charnel house, 1399 found dead in the streets.

29 September

Busy day everything gone wrong today, machine stopped, belt breaking & everything gone wrong but we might have a better day tomorrow, let us be thankful. We went to Hipperholme to see some friends.

30 September

Exit Summer.

1 October

Clocks put back today 1 hour. 10 Zeppelins raid England tonight. One brought down in flames. All the crew perish, awful & overwhelming spectacle.

2 October

Sorry to hear of the death of Mr Fred Wood, only son of George Wood, West Vale, he was called up a few weeks ago, he was medically unfit when called up, but he was passed. Ever since his entry he has been in hospital, & when compelled to do physical work he broke down & collapsed, I call this murder. Weather somewhat broken just now.

4 October

Will bought a portable typewriter, "Corona" a very useful machine. He can work it very well. I have started to write my autobiography with it & up to the present have had to take a lot of ridicule, but I don't care it amuses me. All our folks at Blackpool, PC from Bertha. Price of mushrooms today 1/8 if you please.

5 October

Picture House tonight to see my old favourite play "Caste" featuring Sir John Hare As "Old Eccles", it was very good.

6 October

Wet Weather.

7 October

Ma went to Blackpool this morning, our folks are there, a change will do her good but the weather looks bad. The Theatre Royal Harrison Freuin Opera Co, "Rigoletto" afternoon, a capital performance the principles were all very capable artists and it was very enjoyable I had never seen it before.

8 October

Busy morning Mr N Farrar came to dinner & in the evening called again with some lady friends, who entertained us with some music. Will went back with them to Huddersfield for the night.

9 October

Submarines are again doing us heavy losses in ships this last few days freights might well be going up.

10 October

German U boat again crossed to America & outside the 3 mile limit sank 6 or 8 of our ships.

11 October

M J came home today she having enjoyed her holiday, but the weather has been rough, good sea & high winds.

Greek Fleet taken over by the Allies It having been discovered that with the German aid/submarines soon going to upset our plans but the King of Greece will probably lose his crown thro this at last, I hope so.

12 October

Wild wet weather. Bought Coaching Days in Yorkshire by Tom Bradley, a most interesting book on the coaching days, details of all the coaches in & out of all Yorkshire Towns 3/-.

13 October

West Vale in the morning.

14 October

High wind with heavy rain.

15 October

Quiet day. Late in the morning Norman Farrar came, he goes to Birmingham tomorrow to enlist, we are all so sorry, we shall miss him.

Walter came in and we had some music, most enjoyable. Norman stayed with us all night, it was too late to run him home.

16 October

Harvey came this morning to spend the day with us, Will went with him to Halifax evening.

Sam Bairstow died Oct 15th, a well known character in Elland, Cask Dealer etc, a noisy follower of Football. Known him all my life, lived at Salterhebble in his earlier days and was never fond of work, but managed to get on in the world.

17 October

Harvey left for home 8.30. No striking news from the front, only we are slowly pushing the Huns back.

18 October

Unsettled day. Greece at last is now in the Allies hands and will have to do what the powers want. Germans are taking this move very badly according to the papers.

Sailly-Saillisel a very strong German position & of great importance, taken by the English & the French & firmly held, in fact this week we have slowly pushed them back on the whole line.

19 October

Another old friend gone today Alfred Speak West Vale died today he was well respected in the neighbourhood, generous giver to St John's when the church was built. He also gave the Organ, the Drinking Fountain he erected in commemoration of the Diamond Jubilee 1897. For a long time he has been in delicate health. Formerly we were very friendly but latterly with removing got out of touch.

21 October

Attended the funeral of Mr Alfred Speak Greetland Church, it was largely attended I saw many old friends there. Harvey came again today for the weekend, they went to theatre to see "My Lady Frayle".

Knowing him from youth he was not one to go out of his way for someone's help, he must have some popular cause. He was always a sly dog & delighted to get somebody over the line & then degrade them. I could quote scores of cases, he always wore an Imperial demeanour with only a few selected friends. He was unknown to the outside world.

22 October

All stayed at home today.

23 October

Harvey went home today. Very busy today. What with this depression & anxiety one cannot stand this constant strain much longer.

24 October

Fall of Constanta, Romanians retire, this is decidedly unpleasant to the Allies.

25 October

Today's news. Verdun Triumph. Fort Vaux almost encircled, great haul of prisoners & booty, a great French Victory they are now back in the position they occupied on Feb 24th.

Harry Lauder the Scotch Comic Singer according to the "Star" took £1,100 as his share of the taking, this works out at £88,400 a year. According to his own statement he still has contracts to fulfil which bring him in considerable less than £100 a week. What about the Prime Minister and other

members of National Importance? I think we are as Carlyle said. A nation of D.... Fools.

Our Allies pushing forward on the Somme.

26 October

Naval fight in the Channel. 10 or 12 German Destroyers made their appearance & an action took place, we drove them off, sinking 2 of their ships, while we lost 1 & another had to be beached.

27 October

Cold showery weather. West Vale at night but very difficult getting about, no lights of any description make it very dangerous.

28 October

Will went to Birmingham with Mr Norman Farrar for the week end and the latter is in a Flying School there.

29 October

Showery all day. Spent the day with Mrs Varden Dickens. Hx Lecture Mr Bellamy on "Holland" it was a splendid lecture.

30 October

Fearful wild wet day in fact it has never ceased since. Had the greatest difficulty to get home tonight. Will got home tonight about 8.30 he had not enjoyed his outing so much on account of the bad weather. Norman was very well and settling down to his work.

31 October

Better day. Heavy fighting still going on. Another order out to Exemption Committee to pass all young men into the Army but those of exceptional occupations. This is giving us very serious trouble and will be a very hard fight at the next Tribunal for our boy. This tension is becoming unbearable, they are assuming a very grave aspect.

1 November

Wet all day.

2 November

French & Italians have made a desperate dash at the enemy and have inflicted on them heavy losses and captured many prisoners & guns. Verdun is now almost clear. The Germans are desperate at their failure here as terrific loss of life to them.

3 November

British & Neutral ships are still falling the pray of German submarines, this is becoming a very serious question.

4 November

Beautiful day. Will took Ma for a run over the Moors. I went to Huddersfield afternoon for a book "Parish Clerk". I bought a hare they looked so tempting.

5 November

Dull day. Norman came in the afternoon. They went to Hx but could not get into Lecture so came back stayed all night.

6 November

Wet all day. French have done good work last few days. But weather is very much against them. Poor tommies up to their waist in puddles.

7 November

Jugged Hare to Dinner it was a nice change. Mr & Mrs Leary came down this morning stayed supper, we had a most enjoyable time. He always brings some books for me & I return the compliment. He is a regular book worm and I like them to come.

8 November

Still showery. Loss of another P&O steamer in the Mediterranean, but all were saved excepting 3 lives, she had a valuable cargo, this pirate work is getting very serious for us. Collision in the Irish Channel between the LNWR steamer the "Connemara" & the

"Retriever", only a few lives saved, the former boat I crossed over in my visit to Grenore several years ago she was a very fine boat.

9 November

Huddersfield tonight called at a Fishmongers asked the price of "Kippers", 6d per pair, if they go on they will become an aristocratic dish.

Coley tonight to see Dr Jowett, we found him with a bad cold & run down, this bleak parish is very trying for him, a large number of his parishioners have fallen in the war & he has had a most anxious time, Mrs Jowett's place is sorely missed & Miss Jowett has taken on work at St Lukes Hospital, helping the wounded soldiers. Showery all day. We had a very heavy day at the mill, & both Will & myself were quite done up when we finished 6.45.

10 November

Today we had two wounded soldiers to tea, when Will was coming from Birmingham the other week a wounded soldier got into the same compartment & in conversation he said he was coming to Halifax so Will took an interest in him. He had been thru all the principal battles Loos, Neuve Chappelle and the great push. He promised to call at the Infirmary and take him a ride on the sidecar but the weather has not been fit so he wrote for him to come down here so he did & brought another wounded comrade with him. The man's name is Jones & he hails from Birmingham, the other friend came from Salford. So they came to tea & we gave them a good time & they enjoyed themselves and were very nice indeed. They intend coming to see us again, they will be very welcome. They have done their bit.

11 November

Harvey telephoned for Will to go spend the week and he was delayed in the afternoon, so he went over in the sidecar. I went for company, it was very dark over Buckstones and very weird, but we got there alright. I went straight to the Station & was back home by 8 o'clock, we did not leave here 4.45.

12 November

Home all day. We were all tired with our exertions of last week. Will could not get home tonight, he broke down at Delph and went back to Harvey's.

13 November

Better weather. Will landed back early this evening, he soon got his machine right.

14 November

Great Battle in the West proceeding so the reports say this morning. American Election, Dr Wilson elected again so we can expect nothing from him to help us to beat these murderous Huns.

15 November

Our Airmen have been very active at the front this last few days, done a lot of damage to the Germans. Will got his machine repaired & ran back in good time this morning.

16 November

Great Battle, Beaumont Hamel which the Germans have been fortifying since the war started, there we have shattered & driven them all out, 6000 prisoners captured, for the first time the Germans admit this loss, all honour to our brave troops for each victory.

17 November

Frosty today. Germans tried to take back the position they lost yesterday but the French gave them a terrible blow and they had to fall back with great slaughter.

First fall of snow today. "Matinee", Theatre Royal Hx with M J to see the celebrated actor Arthur Bourchier in "Find the Woman" a splendid Co and we were delighted with the charming acting of every member of the cast we came away with a wish to see him again, it was his first visit here.

Will got a Gramophone with a number of records, some very good ones amongst the lot. Coon & Rag Time items are very good, also some of the old standard songs, it's a wonderful invention, in these depressing times it will make us cheer up somewhat.

We can have music to our meals if we choose, kippers go down a little better with a little Music.

19 November

Incessant snow & sleet all day. We had the Gramophone going to cheer us up somewhat.

20 November

Will at home all day bad attack of Colic made him very poorly. Two of our old workpeople who have been to the front & done their bit,

Wilfred Hoyle & Stanley....... from Brighouse, the latter had part of his skull fractured so he is discharged.

21 November

Fall of Monastir, bitter blow for Bulgaria.

22 November

Bitter day today as regards Weather. Sad news comes to hand today.

The Huns with their usual callous brutality have torpedoed the Hospital Ship the "Britannic" in the Aegean Sea she was the world's largest ship, she had 6000 cots. Joe Noble came on this evening we gave him a few selections on the Gramophone he was much amused.

23 November

Dull day rained towards night. Will went to be sworn in at the Drill Hall for the National Motor Service Volunteers.

The National Motor Service Volunteers were part of the Volunteer Training Corps, the Great War equivalent of the Home Guard. They transported men coming home on leave from the railway stations to their homes.

24 November

War news very scant just now. Government now taking control of the flour, no white flour to be had in another few weeks, we go onto Standard Bread, well I don't think this will make us any worse.

25 November

Restful afternoon & Evening. Expected our Bertha but we were disappointed. Will went to Hx with Norman to see "Betty" but it was a frost.

Sir D Haigh on the success of the Battle of Somme. In addition to ground won and heavy casualties inflicted on the enemy the British between July 1st & Nov 18 captured

Prisoners	*38,000*
Heavy Guns	*29*
Field Guns & Howitzers	*96*
Trench Guns	*136*
Machine guns	*514*

A French semi official report puts the enemy losses in men on the Somme at 700,000.

26 November

Had a walk in the morning round Tag Lock this is a favourite walk but bird life was quiet, I only saw a green plover. Norman came to tea & stayed overnight. Mrs Eastwood Hilda & George came on in the evening so we passed a pleasant time. Frosty morning & biting cold wind all day. My landlord Thomas Brearley died suddenly last night, he was 72 *years of age.*

28 November

Last night about 10 *o'clock we were warned of Zepps, this evening paper informs us that Durham & Norfolk but glad to see that* 2 *of them were brought down in flames.*

29 November

Attended funeral of Mr Thos Brearley, my landlord at Cross Mills, we stopped this afternoon. Will took Ma to Todmorden, came on wet, the machine when it got back was simply plastered with dirt.

Mrs E told us that John Dempster had left ½ a Million, he wanted her very much, but she preferred my old friend John, what changes we see I remember them in very humble circumstances, but have watched their rise & progress.

The trials of the deaf

An old gentleman went out to tea & being deaf was unable to join in the conversation. A kind hearted old lady wanting to make him feel at home said, "do you like bananas", to which he replied ", No; I prefer the old fashioned night shirt".

Speaking of children talking at a very early age it is recorded that Job cursed the day he was born.

Bucharest in peril.

Tino still keeping us on the edge. Why do we hesitate, changes have taken place in the Admiralty, why not in other departments, we are at our darkest hour and we want men now of daring courage. Every day brings some new restrictions in food stuffs, some goods you cannot get for money. Both Allied & Neutral ships are daily sunk this is a terrible loss.

1 December

Dull foggy day, in fact we seem to be in fog altogether things begin to look very serious and this depression is having its effect on the people, this toll of lives is terrible to bear.

2 December

Went to Greetland with flowers for Arnold then forward to Halifax to have my hair cut at Mr Days, nobody can cut my hair like he can. M J went to Mrs Eastwoods. Norman came back late in the evening & stayed all night with us.

Papers today report the Will of the late Alfred Speak £75,000 odd I do not see he has left his sister, Mrs Eastwood, anything which I consider mean. I see he makes a flutter by giving money to persons who have been in his employ for 10 years, well £100 will clear that lot off. I was not surprised at the amount, he got all his Fathers, Harry's and got John Ely's, in fact he collared the lot, we know latterly he has been generous but when you have a surfeit of money, is not like generosity with a moderate pocket.

3 December

Walter Greenwood came into tell us his father had died suddenly, he married my cousin Mary Hannah. We had a restful day, as far as labour was concerned but the hanging suspense of the Tribunal hanging over our head & the black look out of the country is getting on our nerves.

4 December

Will helping Ma to make the Xmas Cake.

6 December

Grave Political Crisis

The Prime Minister (Mr Asquith) has tendered his resignation to the King. I am afraid there is something behind all this, we are getting into desperate straits my belief, and it will take nothing short of a miracle to get us out.

Food Control

Hotels & Restaurants are forbidden by law, to have more than 3 courses for dinner at most. This will be a shock to some people but it won't be a disappointment to me I consider that this is quite enough for anybody.

Bucharest in the hands of the Huns. This is a great blow to the Allied Powers. Germans have taken possession of the grain and oil fields which they are in great need of.

7 December

Lloyd George to form a Cabinet, if we have one man at the head of affairs with force I think L George will fill the place to the nations credit and I wish him the best of luck.

9 December

Afternoon went to Huddersfield to hear O'Mara Opera Co in Faust, the principals were in excellent hands, it was very fine indeed, the Orchestra was very fine, it gave me great pleasure.

Marquerite Miss Annie Lindsey

Siebal	*Miss Irene Ainsley*
Marthe	*Miss McCarthy*
Fauste	*Mr Wm Boland*
Valentin	*Mr Albert Kirkman*
Mephistophiles	*Mr Joseph Griffin*
Wagner	*Mr Ryan*

10 December

Walk round Copley & up North Dean Wood. Evening went to Birchencliffe Church.

11 December

Heavy dark fog all day, we never had gas out at the mill all day.

Lloyd George Cabinet (War)

Mr Henderson

Mr Bonar Law

Lord Curzon

Lord Milner

12 December

Startled by Peace Proposals by Germany. She wants her colonies back & to retain her Navy & pay no war indemnity, very cool request. Like a gambler he wants to leave the table with his winnings. But no he will have to play the game out. My opinion it's a sign of weakness, he knows his doom. The Allied Powers will treat such offering with contempt.

Dull foggy weather. No news from the front, the weather is too severe, snow & rain, the poor soldiers must feel this ordeal very badly.

14 December

Highest price for flour for 60 years, 87/-.

Sent Joe a P.C

15 December

Good news this morning. Great Victory for the French at Verdun attacking on a 6 mile front broke thru the enemy lines at all points & advanced 2 miles, over 7500 prisoners, including 200 officers were passed to the rear.

HIS MASTERS BREATH

16 December

British advance in Mesopotamia. Cold, frosty day. Went to Huddersfield afternoon. Xmas fare looks very scanty. Turkeys, Geese are too expensive to be popular.

17 December

Will went to Huddersfield this afternoon, Norman came back with him.

18 December

More news coming through about the great battle at Verdun the Germans lost 2 divisions. Well might Gen Nivelle describe it as an excellent day.

19 December

Heavy fall of snow this morning and continued until 11 o'clock.

20 December

Germany is now wanting peace but on her own terms. Today with the ground being all snow bound we had quite a number of birds. Blackbirds, thrushes and Tits etc, and of course the Ancient Briton the Sparrow, so I gave them all the scrap crusts I could find.

Talk about protection, whatever be the sacrifice involved I should rejoice after the War to see prohibition tariffs clapped on everything Made in Germany. I want to see nothing German, alive, dead, manufactured, unmanufactured in this country again.

Bad weather at the front, operations are much restricted.

21 December

Another trying time is coming on for us, Will is called to the Colours on 4th January. But we are putting in another appeal, we are dreading the ordeal, but I hope we shall be successful.

22 December

Busy day at the mill.

23 December

Finished for the Holidays. We had a busy time today in getting all in for Xmas, shop keepers have no assistants so we were forced to fetch them for ourselves. Will went Huddersfield tonight to Mr Farrars.

24 December

Busy day Mr & Mrs Farrar & family came this afternoon to spend Xmas. We had dinner at 6 o'clock, at 12 o'clock the fun began & we kept up until 4.30.

25 December

In the afternoon we went to Huddersfield to Mr & Mrs Farrars Dinner Party and we had a very enjoyable time. I know it was not a time to enjoy ourselves, but this year of gloom, we tried if only for a short time to be happy once more. We stayed the night there & we were made very happy & comfortable, we came home by the 9.45 car I wish everybody could have had a time like it.

27 December

Started work this morning but as usual, a poor muster turned up. It would have been the same if we had played a week, they would have wanted more.

Mr Farrar is a typical Yorkshireman. I was much interested with some of his vernacular sayings Viz There's nowt wrong with right folk.

Our Dinner passed off well, the usual drinks, after that we had some music vocal & instrumental. One of the ladies gave some capital recitations with piano accompaniment. Mr Farrar & M J & Mr Greenwood (Master) played the violin, and I contributed songs etc, & talked up the chimney etc etc which made them laugh. We cleared the room and danced, and we all enjoyed it very much. The Gramophone came in very well for dancing Mr F brought all his Master Records, songs by all the finest Artists in the World they were marvellous we could not have had a better program.

Will had to go to Halifax Barracks this morning to be medically examined & was passed for General Service.

28 December

Downpour all day. M J went to Todmorden to see our folks. Received a letter from Mrs Wm Maude to say her husband was not so well, much depressed at the loss of his brother, Mr Speak, she says he has gout in his hands, & afraid he cannot paint again I sincerely hope this is not the case. Saw the new Moon tonight not thro glass I hope this is luck.

30 December

Dull cold day.

Printed in Great Britain
by Amazon

67419269R00137